A
CHINESE
VIEW
OF
CHINA

JOHN
GITTINGS

BRITISH BROADCASTING CORPORATION

Published by the British Broadcasting Corporation,
35 Marylebone High Street, London W1M 4AA

ISBN 0 563 12408 3

First published 1973
© John Gittings 1973

Printed in England by Jolly & Barber Ltd, Rugby, Warwickshire.

This book was published simultaneously with a BBC Radio Series, *China – Change and Continuity in the World's Longest Surviving Civilisation.* The radio series, presented by Richard Harris and produced by Adrian Johnson, was first broadcast on Radio 3 on Mondays and Thursdays from 2 April to 5 July 1973.

CONTENTS

INTRODUCTION

Even the most sympathetic interpretations of China need to be supplemented by listening directly to what the Chinese themselves have to say. The purpose of *A Chinese View of China* is to provide an opportunity for doing this, through the thirty-four extracts from various Chinese writers which have been selected in order to illustrate some of the main features of their history and society. The series of extracts, each preceded by a short explanatory note, is followed by a reference section where the reader can find some basic information of a mostly factual kind and some suggestions for further reading.

Of course there is more than one 'Chinese view of China', and by making this particular selection of translations rather than another, I have tilted the balance of interpretation a particular way. And it seems both logical and necessary to present an interpretation which by and large reflects the kind of attitudes towards their past and their present which are held by the Chinese in China today, rather than the attitude of any other Chinese at different places or at different times. (It is also an interpretation which I myself generally share.)

It is logical to look at the Chinese view of China, because they are Chinese and it is their own country and their own history. It is necessary to make what is perhaps a special effort to see the Chinese point of view, because on the whole we have not paid enough attention to it in the past. Indeed there have been many occasions over the last century and a half of regular contact between China and the West when the prevailing attitude towards China revealed more about ourselves than about the Chinese.

The Western view of China has taken many different shapes and forms in modern times, and it is in a state of change again today. In the nineteenth century China appeared to some observers as a civilisation unmatched in age and achievement, to others as a country crippled by tradition and ripe for Christian salvation. After the 1911 Revolution China was seen as a brave experiment – but then as a dismal failure – in Western-style democracy. During the war with Japan, the Chinese were first ignored while they fought alone, then eulogised as stout little allies in the East, and finally written off for not having tried hard enough. Then came the civil war and the communist victory of 1949, which led to the building of a revolutionary society in China which so disturbed the government of the United States that it tried to pretend that it did not exist. After more than twenty years of, for the most part, mystification and mis-understanding about China, President Nixon reversed American policy and visited Peking, allowing millions of television viewers to discover for themselves that the Chinese were human, and that the Chinese brand of socialism might not be such a bad thing after all.

Whenever we look at the society of another country, we do so through a glass which also partly reflects the political and social contours of our own country. But it seems likely that in the case of China our view has been more than usually distorted. There are a number of reasons for this. The very distance of China from the West made it seem more mysterious and 'inscrutable' from the start. Then it became very difficult to see what was happening clearly through the dust which was raised by the scramble of the imperialist powers to dismember China. Our view of China was also warped by fairly widespread feelings of racialist contempt mixed up with half-suppressed fears of the Yellow Peril. Racialism is not wholly a thing of the past either. It flourishes, for example, in the British colony of Hongkong where the Chinese are still treated as second-class citizens, and one can also detect its influence behind some of the arguments often heard in the West about China's population (is it a 'threat'?) and China's foreign policy (is it 'expansionist'?).

Finally, the fact that the Chinese revolution was successfully completed under communist leadership, arousing such sustained hos-tility from the United States and to a great extent from its Western allies, meant that our view of socialist China was now distorted by a considerable degree of cold-war bias. It was often very difficult to dis-entangle anti-Chinese propaganda from genuine scholarly writing and research about China, especially in the 1950s and early 1960s. The improvement in political relations since then between China and the West has made it easier for more serious and sympathetic work to be done, but we still have quite a long way to catch up.

I hope that this book will help even slightly to bridge this political and cultural gap in our understanding, and that it will be of some use to readers who are beginning to ask their own questions about China. Not that it will necessarily answer all the questions, but it should at least provide some sort of 'feel' for the Chinese perspective without which any answers are meaningless. The extracts which I have chosen are reasonably comprehensive, but there are some gaps and I have not attempted to provide a dogged dynasty-by-dynasty account of Chinese history. I have tried instead to offer a panoramic, perhaps impressionistic, view of China through Chinese eyes by making a selection of extracts which are as lively and varied as possible. Reading about imperial and modern China should be fun more often than it is, and this applies just as much to China since 1949 where they have not, contrary to some reports, 'abolished' the family, or sex, or laughter. (See, for example, the love scene in Extract 27. Fiction today is rather more serious-minded than it was fifteen years ago when this novel was written, but the style may change again, and in any case I am sure that young men in Chinghsi village still take their girl-friends to the brick-kiln on the southern slope.)

At the same time China *is* a different society with different ideals and social goals from those of the capitalist countries of the West, and no useful purpose is served by trying to pretend that the Chinese are 'just like us', even if they are similar in many respects. Intense political struggle, sometimes leading to violence, has been an important part of the mechanism which has driven the Chinese revolution forward from the early years of land reform (Extract 24) to the Cultural Revolution (Extracts 30–3). And while everyday life for the Chinese has much in common with our own, the forms of social organisation and (much more important) the collective spirit behind them is altogether another matter (Extract 34).

But reading about China, especially the China of the past, can also be a very disturbing experience. Against the art and the culture of imperial China one has to off-set the oppression and suffering of millions of common folk whose real situation only emerges infrequently from the official version provided in the dynastic histories – fiction and poetry often provide a more truthful account (see Extracts 5 and 6, and the suggestions for further reading on pp. 184–5). Reading about modern China during the past century of economic and social upheaval can be even more disturbing because so much of the damage was caused by the countries to which we ourselves belong and by the economic forces which still shape our own lives. How many of those, for example, who held shares in a famous tobacco company in the 1930s could have had any conception of the plight of the tobacco leaf producer in eastern Shantung province (Extract 20)?

All these considerations are very relevant to a proper understanding of the Chinese view of their own history, and as a glance at the list of acknowledgements and sources at the end of this book will show, I have made full use of post-1949 writings from China to interpret this view. The quality of English-language magazines like *China Reconstructs* and *Chinese Literature*, and the choice of books translated into English available from Peking, has fluctuated over the years, but standards which have been generally high are improving again after the Cultural Revolution when they went through a very bad patch. It is well worth putting one's name on the mailing-list of one of the bookshops which handles publications from Peking, and subscribing to one of these magazines (see p. 205).

Every book on China has to have a technical note about the system of transliteration which the author has decided to use, or not as the case may be. Here it is. I have left the transcription of Chinese words and names as they are in the various extracts, without bothering about consistency. I have used the standard but old-fashioned Wade-Giles in the sections written by myself, without bothering about apostrophes. I could have adopted *Hanyu Pinyin*, the relatively new phonetic system developed in China, which is widely used for language teaching and appears in a few recent Western books. On balance it is a better system too. But this would have meant changing absolutely everything, including all the extracts from the books and magazines published in Peking, which themselves have not got around to using *Hanyu Pinyin* yet. Either way has its disadvantages. Scholars get very upset about this business of transcription, but the general reader need not worry so much.

Formal acknowledgements come later on, but here I would like to thank specially Andrew Watson and Michael Yahuda for reading the manuscript, Richard and Sally Greenhill for supplying their photographs on China today, and Paul Clifford for guiding me to the sources of many of the earlier illustrations. The cover picture was taken by the Greenhills in the gardens of the Lintung hot springs resort near Sian (where Chiang Kai-shek was arrested by his own officers in December 1936 and persuaded to start fighting the Japanese instead of the Communists). The girl's umbrella is made of paper and varnished with oil from the *tung* tree. The back cover is taken from a picture-sized paper-cut showing life in the countryside, with a column of Red Guards marching by on their way to see Chairman Mao in Peking.

TRANSLATIONS
FROM
THE
CHINESE

'Battle on the bridge' between two feudal armies. *Part of a 2nd-century AD stone slab carving*

IMPERIAL CHINA
Continuity and Change

1 A FEUDAL OFFICER'S COMPLAINT

China's recorded history begins in the eighth century BC, with a dozen or so small feudal states clustered around the basin of the Yellow River. For more than five hundred years these warring states struggled intermittently for supremacy until the first unified China was established at the end of the third century BC. During this period many of the distinctive features of Chinese culture and art, philosophy and political thought, were already being formed. All the traditional Chinese 'classics' date from this time; one of the earliest is the *Book of Songs*, a collection of poems and folk-songs. In China today its anonymous authors are praised for the way that they have depicted the injustices of the feudal society. In this poem a junior official in one of the states complains that some have to work much harder than others.

'The Northern Hills'

I climb the northern hills
Picking the boxthorn.[1]
Zealous officials
Must labour day and night;
The king's business is endless,
Causing our parents worry for their sons.

Everywhere under the sky
Is the king's dominion;
To the uttermost ends of the earth
All men are his servants;
But the tasks are unequal
And I have more work than the rest.

[1]The boxthorn is used for medicinal purposes, and its collection by Red Army soldiers nearly three thousand years later is described in Extract 22.

A team of four gallops on and on,
The king's business is unending;
I am congratulated on my youth.
Complimented on my vigour;
While my muscles are strong
I have business on every hand.

Some men rest idle at home,
Others wear themselves out in the service of the state;
Some lie quiet in bed,
Others are always on the move;

Some have never heard weeping or wailing,
Others toil without rest;
Some loll at ease,
Others are harassed working for the king;

Some take pleasure in wine,
Others have no respite from care;
Some just go round airing their views,
Others are left with all the work.

2 THE TYRANT WHO FOUNDED A DYNASTY

China is well known for the length and continuity of its imperial history and culture – the dynastic period lasted officially from 221 BC when China was first unified to AD 1911 when the Manchu empire was overthrown. But length does not mean stability; for roughly one-third of this 2000-year imperial span China was divided or at war or suffering from famine and rebellion. Each new dynasty was established by force of arms, either by foreign invaders or domestic usurpers, and usually with a blood-bath of the survivors of the previous dynasty. The challenger often took advantage of popular unrest or rebellion to hoist himself into power, and the Chinese have a saying that, 'He who fails is a bandit; he who succeeds is a king'.

The next extract paints an irreverent picture of someone who only succeeded for a few years. Chu Wen, Lord of Liang, finished off the 'glorious' Tang dynasty which had been in decline for over a hundred years, and set up the Later Liang dynasty in AD 907. This led in turn to fifty years of disunity known as the period of the Five Dynasties, although there were no less than eleven claimants to the throne. In the following Sung dynasty the writer Chang Chi-hsien wrote a popular history of the Five Dynasties, and in this extract from it he describes how the Lord of Liang attracted sycophantic scholars and courtiers around him as he climbed to power. (If the Lord of Liang's new dynasty had been longer-lived, Chang Chi-hsien would have had to describe him instead as a wise ruler and a patron of the arts.)

'Tyrant and Scholars' by Chang Chi-hsien

The founder of the dynasty of Liang was notorious for his ferocity, cruelty and tyranny. After he had unified the four principal military districts under his single command, he was feared as if he was the king of beasts. Anyone in his service who incurred his displeasure in the slightest degree would be immediately beheaded. When the officials of Liang left their homes in the morning to go to court, they would bid eternal farewell to their kin, and when they returned safe and sound in the evening, the whole family would rejoice – so uncertain were they of their lives. His guests, when they were received in audience, trembled as if from bitter wintry cold.

A doctor of literature by the name of Tu Hsun-ho sought service under the Lord of Liang, requesting an interview. His card was presented by an attendant, but His Lordship gave no indication whatever of his pleasure. As a result, Tu was kept waiting for several months in his inn. For the rule was that the innkeeper must not permit any guest to depart, once his name had been registered at the palace for an audience, though he might have stayed for as long as a year, suffering from cold and hunger in his lodgings. Otherwise, the hotel-keeper was liable to meet with serious trouble in case the guest should at last be summoned to court and not be present.

Tu went daily to the palace waiting-room for news of the audience. One morning His Lordship was sitting in his reception room and enquired of his retainers where Tu was, and they replied that he was present in the waiting-room. Before he could be summoned, however, some important personage arrived on horseback at the

Two Sons of Heaven: above, Emperor Cheng Tsung (1295–1308) of the 'barbarian' Mongol dynasty – he came after Kublai Khan – and right, Emperor Shen Tsung (1573–1620) of the Ming dynasty which restored Chinese rule

palace, and was immediately received by His Lordship. When the guest departed, it was already after noon and His Lordship retired to his private apartments.

Tu became very hungry, so he asked the usher's permission to return to the inn, but the officer refused his request and hastily arranged a meal for him instead. 'You must have some pity on our lives,' he explained, 'for if His Lordship should send for you when you are away, that would mean the end of our days.'

After dusk the Lord of Liang appeared once more in his reception hall and asked for dice, which he threw again and again on the table, as if he used them to decide some irresolution. Somehow or other he was not satisfied with the results of his throws, for he glared around at his retinue, who trembled with fear.

Finally His Lordship, holding the six dice in his palm, shouted 'Tu Hsin-ho!' and threw them once more on the table. All six ivory cubes turned up with the red four, and the poor scholar-guest was commanded to make his appearance.

The usher led him in, warning him to walk fast, which he did to such good purpose that he involuntarily reached the steps of the dais. His Lordship loudly rebuked him for coming so close to his throne, which made the scholar burst into a cold sweat, mumbling at the same time 'Yes, Sire! Yes, Sire!' After expressing his honour and gratefulness at being received, he was permitted to take a seat.

Tu was still trembling with fright and had almost lost his presence of mind, when His Lordship graciously remarked that he had long heard of the scholar's name, upon which the guest rose from his chair and wanted to fall on his knees to express his appreciation.

'That's unnecessary,' roared His Lordship. Tu bowed profoundly and resumed his seat.

The Lord of Liang looked beyond to the courtyard, and observed to the attendants that raindrops seemed to be falling. They went obsequiously out of the hall to see and returned confirming the fact, though when they raised their heads they did not notice the presence of a single cloud. The drops were, moreover, heavy ones, and as they struck the eaves, one could hear the sound. His Lordship got down from his dais to have a look himself, returning after a minute or two to his seat.

'Have you, sir, ever seen rain falling without the presence of clouds?' he demanded of Tu.

The scholar replied timidly in the negative.

'When there is rain without clouds,' His Lordship laughingly commented, 'it signifies that Heaven is weeping. I wonder what that augurs.'

He commanded that a pen and paper be brought and requested Tu to compose a poem on the theme 'Rain Without Clouds'.

When the scholar first took his seat facing the Lord of Liang, he was embarrassed and felt very uncomfortable, as if he was sitting on burning coals, and now that he was ordered to compose a poem, he dared not refuse. Still keeping his seat, he managed to finish in the twinkling of an eye a poem of four lines which he presented respectfully to His Lordship, who seemed delighted with the composition, inviting him then and there to dinner.

They parted after spending a pleasant evening together, the royal host announcing that he would later give a formal banquet in honour of the guest, who once more bowed his thanks and retired.

His poem, a specimen of impudent flattery and adulation, said in effect that while the Great Universe remained constant and eternal, an exceptional phenomenon had been noted, namely, raindrops impelling themselves on the glowing solar disc; if in this manner brilliant sunshine and rain-laden clouds lost their distinctiveness, such a miraculous freak of nature could owe its birth only to the infinite creative powers of His Lordship!

From that time on Tu became a court favourite.

On his return to the inn he felt ill from fright and nervousness, suffering so severely from diarrhoea that he could hardly rise on his feet. The court usher watched at the bedside and attended to the medical requirements as if he were a loving parent. The next day another official came to announce that the Lord of Liang desired to receive him again, and urged him to proceed quickly on horseback to the palace. Left with no alternative, he made his toilet and mounted his steed with great difficulty, finding on his arrival that some five or six others had also been summoned. As he was very weak from his ailment, he was among the last to enter the audience hall.

'Mr Tu excelled himself in emphasising in his poem my creative powers,' shouted the lord as soon as he laid eyes on his guest.

This eulogy made Tu so proud that he forgot his illness, and almost running towards the dais, and prostrating himself on the floor to thank His Lordship for the compliment.

The lord had a special mansion prepared for Tu and bestowed on him clothes, money and many other gifts, treating him with particular generosity.

Another scholar from Fukien, who failed in the government

examinations, presented a literary composition to His Lordship on the theme 'Passing Through the Suburbs of the Liang Capital', which impressed him deeply with the ability of the author.

'The rulers of old when rewarding scholars,' declared His Lordship, 'used to say "each word is worth a thousand taels of silver." Unfortunately, my military treasury is burdened with innumerable expenditures, so I can compensate the author only at the rate of one roll of silk for each word.'

The article in question embodied a conversation between the writer and the country elders, who were made to lavish words of fulsome praise on the lord. He also was invited to reside at the government hostel, besides receiving other courtesies.

Later when the Lord of Liang was burning with ambition to become emperor, he sought for scholars and retainers more honest and truthful than those already in his service. One day he and a number of his retinue went into the country ten miles beyond the city gate, and sat in the shade of a large willow tree, the trunk of which required the outstretched arms of many men to encircle, the branches being so luxuriant and wide spreading as to give shelter to some three score of men. He and his followers all rested under the same tree.

'What a magnificent willow tree!' he muttered, as if to himself, and looked around at his suite.

'What a magnificent willow tree!' they all repeated, rising from their seats.

'Its timber can well be used to build carts,' asserted then the Lord of Liang.

Again, it was echoed by the obsequious followers. Only one person differed:

'Although I admit that the tree is a very fine willow,' he said, 'for making carts one should really employ the wood of elm.'

'What a lot of yes-men have we here,' shouted the lord. 'You people like to flatter and deceive me by repeating whatever I say. How can the wood of the willow be used for making carts? One must in fact use that of the elm. But you said the other thing simply because I did so. I used to read with some doubt the anecdote of the state minister who pointed to a deer and called it a horse and all his sycophants agreed with him. I can now readily believe the story!'

Calling to his guards he yelled: 'What are you waiting for? Off with their despicable heads!' Some half hundred powerful men seized those who had repeated that the willow tree would make carts, charged them with wilful and shameless deceit, and slew them.

The founder of the Liang dynasty commended life as a bandit, and was by nature persistent, ambitious and suspicious, much more so than the other heroes of old. He was, moreover, self-willed, audacious and determined in character. It was surely no mere luck or accident that he founded a kingdom and created a dynasty.

3 THE SAGE TEACHES HOW TO BE A BENEVOLENT DESPOT

The Confucian doctrine, which was accepted in some form as the ruling ideology by most dynasties in imperial China, was based as much on the thoughts of Mencius as on those of Confucius. Mencius lived in the fourth century BC during the period of the Warring States, more than 200 years after Confucius, and his teachings are more fully recorded. He has been called a 'tender-minded' Confucianist; in his view the Emperor only enjoyed the 'mandate of heaven' if he won his people's confidence and practised good government. Mencius tried to describe a rationalised form of feudalism, at a time of chronic war and unrest, which would satisfy both the rulers and the ruled, but he was never in any doubt that 'the king should rule and the peasant should till'. The essence of his political philosophy is conveyed in the last paragraph of this extract. According to tradition Mencius was a wandering philosopher who moved from one rival feudal state to another in search of a royal patron who would heed his advice and give him lodging. Here he is talking to King Hsüan of Ch'i, one of his more willing listeners. Note his masterly use of argument by analogy to demonstrate that while the King has the potential to be a virtuous ruler he has failed so far to 'make the effort'. He finds it easier to have compassion for an ox being led to slaughter before his eyes, than for the people outside who want peace.

From Mencius, Book I, *translated by D. C. Lau*

King Hsüan of Ch'i asked, 'Can you tell me about the history of Duke Huan of Ch'i and Duke Wen of Chin?'

'None of the followers of Confucius,' answered Mencius, 'spoke of the history of Duke Huan and Duke Wen. It is for this reason that no one in after ages passed on any accounts, and I have no knowledge of them. If you insist, perhaps I may be permitted to tell you about becoming a true King.'

'How virtuous must a man be before he can become a true King?'

'He becomes a true King by bringing peace to the people. This is something no one can stop.'

'Can someone like myself bring peace to the people?'

'Yes.'

'How do you know that I can?'

'I heard the following [story about you] from Hu He: "The King was sitting in the upper part of the hall and someone led an ox through the lower part. The King noticed this and said, 'Where is the ox going?' 'The blood of the ox is to be used for consecrating a new bell.' 'Spare it. I cannot bear to see it shrinking with fear, like an innocent man going to the place of execution.' 'In that case, should the ceremony be abandoned?' 'That is out of the question. Use a lamb instead.'" I wonder if this is true?

'It is.'

'The heart behind your action is sufficient to enable you to become a true King. The people all thought that you grudged the expense, but, for my part, I have no doubt that you were moved by pity for the animal.'

'You are right,' said the King. 'How could there be such people? Ch'i may be a small state, but I am not quite so miserly as to grudge the use of an ox. It was simply because I could not bear to see it shrink with fear, like an innocent man going to the place of execution, that I used a lamb instead.'

'You must not be surprised that the people thought you miserly. You used a small animal in place of a big one. How were they to know? If you were pained by the animal going innocently to its death, what was there to choose between an ox and a lamb?'

The King laughed and said, 'What was really in my mind, I wonder? It is not true that I grudged the expense, but I *did* use a lamb instead of the ox. I suppose it was only natural that the people should have thought me miserly.'

Confucius (551–479 BC) as seen seventeen centuries later by the famous Sung dynasty painter Ma Yuan

'There is no harm in this. It is the way of a benevolent man. You saw the ox but not the lamb. The attitude of a gentleman towards animals is this: once having seen them alive, he cannot bear to see them die, and once having heard their cry, he cannot bear to eat their flesh. That is why the gentleman keeps his distance from the kitchen.'

The King said, 'The *Book of Odes* says,

> The heart is another man's,
> But it is I who have surmised it.

This describes you perfectly. For though the deed was mine, when I looked into myself I failed to understand my own heart. You described it for me and your words struck a chord in me. What made you think that my heart accorded with the way of a true King?'

'Should someone say to you, "I am strong enough to lift a hundred *chün*[1] but not a feather; I have eyes that can see the tip of a fine hair but not a cartload of firewood," would you accept the truth of such a statement?'

'No.'

'Why should it be different in your own case? Your bounty is sufficient to reach the animals, yet the benefits of your government fail to reach the people. That a feather is not lifted is because one fails to make the effort; that a cartload of firewood is not seen is because one fails to use one's eyes. Similarly, that peace is not brought to the people is because you fail to practise kindness. Hence your failure to become a true King is due to a refusal to act, not to an inability to act.'

'What is the difference in form between refusal to act and inability to act?'

'If you say to someone, "I am unable to do it," when the task is one of striding over the North Sea with Mount T'ai under your arm, then this is a genuine case of inability to act. But if you say, "I am unable to do it," when it is one of massaging an elder's joints for him, then this is a case of refusal to act, not of inability. Hence your failure to become a true King is not the same in kind as "striding over the North Sea with Mount T'ai under your arm", but the same as "massaging an elder's joints for him".

'Treat the aged of your own family in a manner befitting their venerable age and extend this treatment to the aged of other families; treat your own young in a manner befitting their tender age and

[1] Just under seven kilogrammes.

extend this to the young of other families, and you can roll the Empire on your palm.

'The *Book of Odes* says,

> He set an example for his consort
> And also for his brothers,
> And so ruled over the family and the state.

In other words, all you have to do is take this very heart here and apply it to what is over there. Hence one who extends his bounty can bring peace to the Four Seas; one who does not cannot bring peace even to his own family. There is just one thing in which the ancients greatly surpassed others, and that is the way they extended what they did. Why is it then that your bounty is sufficient to reach animals yet the benefits of your government fail to reach the people?

'It is by weighing a thing that its weight can be known and by measuring it that its length can be ascertained. It is so with all things, but particularly so with the heart. Your Majesty should measure his own heart.

'Perhaps you find satisfaction only in starting a war, imperilling your subjects and incurring the enmity of other feudal lords?'

'No. Why should I find satisfaction in such acts? I only wish to realise my supreme ambition.'

'May I be told what this is?'

The King smiled, offering no reply.

'Is it because your food is not good enough to gratify your palate, and your clothes not good enough to gratify your body? Or perhaps the sights and sounds are not good enough to gratify your eyes and ears and your close servants not good enough to serve you? Any of your various officials surely could make good these deficiencies. It cannot be because of these things.'

'No. It is not because of these things.'

'In that case one can guess what your supreme ambition is. You wish to extend your territory, to enjoy the homage of Ch'in and Ch'u, to rule over the Central Kingdoms and to bring peace to the barbarian tribes on the four borders. Seeking the fulfilment of such an ambition by such means as you employ is like looking for fish by climbing a tree.'

'Is it as bad as that?' asked the King.

'It is likely to be worse. If you look for fish by climbing a tree, though you will not find it, there is no danger of this bringing disasters in its train. But if you seek the fulfilment of an ambition like yours by such means as you employ, after putting all your heart

子路

Three disciples of Confucius. From a 2nd-century AD stone slab

and might into the pursuit, you are certain to reap disaster in the end.'

'Can I hear about this?'

'If the men of Tsou and the men of Ch'u were to go to war, who do you think would win?'

'The men of Ch'u.'

'That means that the small is no match for the big, the few no match for the many, and the weak no match for the strong. Within the Seas there are nine areas of ten thousand li^1 square, and the territory of Ch'i makes up one of these. For one to try to overcome the other eight is no different from Tsou going to war with Ch'u. Why not go back to fundamentals?

'Now if you should practise benevolence in the government of your state, then all those in the Empire who seek office would wish to find a place at your court, all tillers of land to till the land in outlying parts of your realm, all merchants to enjoy the refuge of your market-place, all travellers to go by way of your roads, and all those who hate their rulers to lay their complaints before you. This being so, who can stop you from becoming a true King?'

'I am dull-witted,' said the King, 'and cannot see my way beyond this point. I hope you will help me towards my goal and instruct me plainly. Though I am slow, I shall make an attempt to follow your advice.'

'Only a Gentleman can have a constant heart in spite of a lack of constant means of support. The people, on the other hand, will not have constant hearts if they are without constant means. Lacking constant hearts, they will go astray and fall into excesses, stopping at nothing. To punish them after they have fallen foul of the law is to set a trap for the people. How can a benevolent man in authority allow himself to set a trap for the people? Hence when determining what means of support the people should have, a clear-sighted ruler ensures that these are sufficient, on the one hand, for the care of parents, and, on the other, for the support of wife and children, so that the people always have sufficient food in good years and escape starvation in bad; only then does he drive them towards goodness; in this way the people find it easy to follow him.

'Nowadays, the means laid down for the people are sufficient neither for the care of parents nor for the support of wife and children. In good years life is always hard, while in bad years there is no way of escaping death. Thus simply to survive takes more energy than

---

[1] About a third of an English mile.

the people have. What time can they spare for learning about rites and duty?

'If you wish to put this into practice, why not go back to fundamentals? If the mulberry is planted in every homestead of five mu[1] of land, then those who are fifty can wear silk; if chicken, pigs and dogs do not miss their breeding season, then those who are seventy can eat meat; if each lot of a hundred mu is not deprived of labour during the busy seasons, then families with several mouths to feed will not go hungry. Exercise due care over the education provided by village schools, and discipline the people by teaching them duties proper to sons and younger brothers, and those whose heads have turned grey will not be carrying loads on the roads. When the aged wear silk and eat meat and the masses are neither cold nor hungry, it is impossible for their prince not to be a true King.'

4 A CHINESE TUTANKHAMEN

Museums all over the world contain fine collections of Chinese paintings, ceramics, sculptures and bronze, purchased or looted during the past century of Western penetration in China. After the People's Republic was set up in 1949 all archaeological sites were placed under the control of the State Archaeological Service, the export of antiquities was prohibited, and a number of important new discoveries have been made, each one revealing even more of the wealth and sophistication of Chinese art from the earliest dynasties and before. There was a spate of new finds in the late 1950s when many large-scale irrigation works were being constructed. Ten years later when China started a massive programme of anti-airraid shelter building, more treasures were unearthed. Apart from some minor incidents of vandalism by Red Guards early on in the Cultural Revolution, China's antiquities have been carefully preserved and displayed, often in newly-built provincial

[1] Mu, or mow, about one sixth of an acre.

museums. But exhibits are never presented just for their aesthetic value, and the Chinese attach great significance to archaeology as a means of explaining the social and economic conditions of their past history. The following extract describes the recent discovery (in 1972) of an embalmed body in a 2100-year-old Han dynasty tomb which also contained great quantities of artifacts, including one of the earliest known silk paintings. It also points up the political moral to be learnt from this example of the 'extravagance' of China's feudal rulers.

From China Pictorial, *October 1972*

The body of a woman, wooden coffins and large numbers of burial accessories were found in a good state of preservation inside a 2100-year-old tomb recently unearthed at Mawangtui on the out-skirts of Changsha City, Hunan Province, Central China. The tomb has been identified as belonging to the early Western Han Dynasty (206 BC-AD 24) and is hailed as a rare find of considerable importance.

Changsha is an ancient city with a long history. As early as the Warring States Period (475–221 BC) it was famed for its well-developed iron smelting and casting, textile manufacture and lacquer painting. Its economy further advanced considerably during the Western Han dynasty. The tomb and its contents will contribute greatly to the study of the history, culture, handicrafts and agri-culture as well as medicine and antisepsis of that period. Chinese archaeological workers are at the moment working on the findings.

The body is quite well-preserved. It was half immersed in a reddish fluid and encased in twenty layers of silk clothing. The subcutaneous loose connective tissues are still elastic and the fibres distinct. The colour of its femoral artery is about the same as that in a person newly dead. When preservatives were injected into the soft tissues at the time of excavation, swelling ensued and then subsided gradually. It is estimated that the woman was about fifty when she died.

The tomb is 20 metres deep from the top of the mound to the burial chamber, and is of a very complicated structure. The six layers of coffins are placed one within the other and the whole rests on wooden sleepers. Tightly packed about the walls and the top of the outermost coffin was a 30- to 40-cm-thick charcoal layer weighing more than 10,000 *jin* [a catty or Chinese pound]. The char-coal layer was sealed with white clay, 60 to 130 cm thick. It is prob-

Acrobats. A brick tile design from a Han dynasty tomb in Szechwan

20

ably due to these air-tight layers and other treatment that the corpse, coffins and the large quantity of burial accessories are so free from decay.

More than one thousand burial accessories were found. They include silk fabrics, lacquer ware, bamboo and wooden utensils, pottery, grain, foodstuffs and specially made funerary objects. The silk fabrics are of almost every variety known to the Han Dynasty (206 BC-AD 220), namely, plain silk, gauze, brocade, embroideries and damask. They are of gay variegated patterns and done with exquisite technique.

The most valuable of these is an elaborate painting in colour on silk draping the innermost coffin. It is T-shaped, 205 cm long, 92 cm wide at top and 47.7 cm wide at bottom, with flying ribbons at the corners. It is divided into three parts. The upper horizontal represents heaven. In the upper right corner is a sun containing a golden crow. Below it are a *fusang* tree and eight smaller suns. These were probably inspired by the myth 'Yi the Archer Shoots Down Nine Suns'. In the upper left corner hangs a moon with a toad and a rabbit. Below is the scene 'Lady Chang Ngo Flies to the Moon'. The middle panel shows an old woman, escorted by three handmaids, walking slowly along, leaning on a stick. Before her are two kneeling figures. This is probably a scene from the daily life of the mistress. Below is a feast. At the bottom are scenes of sea and land. A big man stands on two huge fish, holding a flat white object which probably symbolises the earth.

This remarkable work is the first silk painting we have discovered which dates back 2100 years and which combines mythology and real life class distinctions.

There are also more than 180 pieces of lacquer ware, mostly wood-based, nearly all of which have retained their original lustre. They are superbly designed and the painted patterns are extremely diverse, with interwoven lines in exquisite composition. Also in the tomb were many kinds of pottery: tripods, caskets, ewers and square vases. Some of the lacquer ware and pottery held glutinous rice cakes, pickled vegetables, peaches, pears, arbutus, melons and unhusked rice. The food and fruit were easily identified when unearthed.

Wooden figurines, inscribed bamboo-slips and bamboo containers are the three main kinds of wood or bamboo articles found. The bamboo containers held eggs, imitation ivory, and articles made of silk. Among the more valuable are 120 or so wooden figurines, either dressed in coloured silk costumes or painted in different hues, including 26 comprising an orchestra and dance group. Among the musical instruments are a 25-stringed wooden *se* (zither-like instrument), a *yu* (bamboo wind instrument) with 22 pipes of varying lengths arranged in two rows, and a pitch-pipe formed of 12 bamboo pipes.

On the burial accessories were clay seals and inscriptions in ink, the ones reading 'Household Manager of the Marquis of Ta' and the others 'Family of the Marquis of Ta'. According to the *Han Shu (History of the Han Dynasty)* and Szuma Chien's *Shih Chi (Historical Records)* the hereditary title 'Marquis of Ta' was conferred by the Emperor Hui in the second year of his reign (193 BC) and was withdrawn in the fourth generation. The body of the woman discovered is likely the wife of the first Marquis of Ta, Marquis Li Tsang. The Marquis of Ta was a petty noble among the feudal princes in the early years of the Han dynasty, with a fief containing only 700 households. The fact that he deployed so much labour and squandered so much wealth for the burial of his wife is compelling evidence of the extravagance of the feudal rulers and their exploitation of the people.

Chairman Mao has pointed out that in feudal society, 'the peasants and the handicraft workers were the basic classes which created the wealth and culture of this society.' To get the people to know their own history and recognise their own creative power is of primary importance. The funerary articles made with such consummate skill in early Han reflect the ingenuity and skill of the Chinese people. The treasures buried for two thousand years have now been restored to them.

5 THE THOUGHTS OF A REFORMING PRIME MINISTER

The Sung dynasty, which followed the disorderly interregnum of the Five Dynasties (Extract 2), is usually renowned for its painting, scholarship and its civilised emperors. The reforms of Prime Minister Wang An-shih, in the later half of the eleventh century,

康乾版畫(一六六二—一七九五)

插秧

晨雨麥秋潤午風槐
夏涼溪南與溪北笈
歌擁新秧拋擲不停
手左右無亂行我教
插秧馬代勞民莫忘

一五五

耕織圖

Planting out the rice shoots. But rural life was less cheerful in times of 'flood or drought'

remind us that there was a darker side of life for the Chinese peasant, oppressed by debt and inescapably vulnerable to flood or famine. Wang's new policies included pre-harvest state loans to the peasant, price control to discourage speculation, equal land taxation, and the ending of forced labour. The reforms were abandoned on the death of Wang's imperial patron in AD 1085. Wang died a disappointed man a year later, and the record of his reforms was suppressed or distorted by historians who regarded him as a trouble-maker.

'Thoughts', a poem by Wang An-shih

Before ever I took up office
I grieved for the common people;
If a year of plenty cannot fill their bellies
What must become of them in flood or drought?
Though no brigands molest them,
How long can they last out?
Above all they dread the officials
Who ruin eight or nine households out of ten,
For when the millet and wheat fail in the fields
Without money for a bribe they cannot appeal for relief,
And those trudging to town to plead with the magistrate
Are whipped away from his gate.
Worst of all is the season when winter turns to spring,
Killing off the old and frail,
For the district head locks up the granaries
And county officials, cracking whips, levy taxes.
The villagers are squeezed dry,
The southern fields stripped of men,
Yet only a mite of the spoils goes to the state
While treacherous scoundrels prosper.
An official blind to this may rest content
And style himself 'Father and Mother of the People';
But since I came to help govern this poor district
My heart fails me, shame overwhelms me,
For today I am the one responsible
For all that once appalled me.
Even a sage was hard put to it to manage government fields,
And my abilities are of the meanest;
Self-reproach spurs me on to do my best
And I share my worries with my colleagues.

6 THE REBELS TAKE A GIFT BY GUILE

Shortly before the Sung emperors were driven south of the Yangtze by the Kin Tartars from outside the Great Wall, a band of 'brigands' sprang up to the east of the capital, making repeated forays from their base in the marshlands to defeat tens of thousands of government troops. Popular stories about their leader, Sung Chiang, and his thirty-five 'brave men' were soon being recounted by the professional story-tellers in the market-place. Two centuries later (around 1370) a polished version of these epic tales was produced by Shih Nai-an, and he retained much of the story-tellers' vivid colloquial style. This is the novel *Shui Hu Chuan* or *Heroes of the Marshes*, famous ever since for its portrayal of a Robin Hood-type band of heroes each of whom had been unjustly outlawed from society and who struck back jointly at their oppressors. It is the classic traditional novel of peasant revolt, and Mao Tse-tung as a young schoolboy used to read it surreptitiously in class. In this extract, a convoy of precious birthday gifts is being conveyed from a corrupt governor to his father-in-law by a squad of soldiers (disguised for safety as porters) led by Yang Chih, a tough sergeant-major. Yang keeps forcing the pace to avoid an ambush by bandits, but the governor's elderly chief steward who is accompanying the convoy has just encouraged the soldiers to stage a sit-down strike in a cool pine grove. What will befall them as they take their ease? Read on and you shall learn . . .

From chapter 16 of Heroes of the Marshes

Yang Chih was going to reply when he saw a shadowy figure poke his head out of a grove opposite and peer at them. 'What did I tell you?' he shouted. 'Isn't that a bad fellow over there?' Flinging aside his switch, he seized his sword and charged into the grove, shouting: 'Insolent villain! How dare you spy on our convoy?'

In the grove he found a line of seven wheel-barrows and six men, buff naked, resting in the shade. One of them, a fellow with a scarlet birthmark on the side of his temple, grabbed a sword when he saw Yang Chih advancing. The seven men cried in alarm: '*Aiya!*' and leaped to their feet.

'Who are you?' Yang Chih yelled.

'Who are you?' the seven countered.

'Aren't you robbers?'

'That's what we should be asking you! We're only poor merchants. We haven't any money to give you!'

'So you're poor merchants. And I suppose I'm rich!'

'Who are you, really?'

'Tell me first where you're from.'

'We seven are from Haochow. We're bringing dates to sell in the Eastern Capital. At first we hesitated to pass this way because many people say that bandits often rob merchants on Yellow Earth Ridge. But then we said to ourselves: "All we've got are some dates and nothing of any value." So we decided to cross the ridge. Since the weather is so hot, we thought we'd rest in this grove till the cool of evening. When we heard you fellows coming up the rise we were afraid you might be bandits, so we sent this brother out for a look.'

'So that's how it is – only ordinary merchants. I thought he was a robber when I saw him watching us, so I hurried in here to investigate.'

'Please have some dates, sir,' said the seven.

'No, thanks,' replied Yang Chih. Sword in hand, he returned to the convoy.

'Since there are bandits around, we'd better leave!' said the chief steward, who was seated beneath a tree.

'I thought they were bandits, but they're only date merchants,' Yang Chih explained.

'If it were like you said,' the old steward remarked sarcastically, pointing his chin at the porters, 'by now these fellows would all be dead!'

'No need to quarrel,' said Yang Chih. 'I only want everything to go well. You men can rest. We'll march on after it cools down a bit.'

The guards smiled. Yang Chih stabbed the point of his sword into the ground, then he too sat down beneath a tree to rest and cool off.

In less time than it takes to eat half a bowl of rice, another man appeared in the distance. Carrying two buckets on the ends of a shoulder pole, he sang as he mounted the ridge:

> 'Beneath a red sun that burns like fire,
> Half scorched in the fields is the grain.
> Poor peasant hearts with worry are scalded,
> While the rich themselves idly fan!'

Still singing, he walked to the edge of the pine grove, rested his buckets and sat down in the shade of a tree.

'What have you got in those buckets?' the soldiers asked him.

'White wine.'

'Where are you going with it?'

'To the village, to sell.'

'How much a bucket?'

'Five strings of cash – not a copper less.'

The soldiers talked it over. 'We're hot and thirsty. Why not buy some? It will ease the heat in our bodies.' They all began chipping in.

'What are you fellows up to?' Yang Chih shouted, when he noticed what they were doing.

'We're going to buy a little wine.'

Grasping the blade of his sword, Yang Chih flailed them with its hilt and swore. 'What gall! How dare you buy wine without asking me?'

'Always raising a stinking fuss over nothing! It's our money! What is it to you if we buy wine? He beats us for that, too!'

'What do you stupid bastards know anyhow? You see wine and all you can think of is guzzling! But not a thought do you give to all the tricks that are pulled on the road! Do you know how many good men have been toppled by drugs?'

The wine vendor looked at Yang Chih and laughed coldly. 'You don't know much yourself, master merchant! I wasn't going to sell you any in the first place. What a dirty thing to say about a man's wine!'

As they were quarrelling, the date merchants emerged from the grove, swords in hand. 'What's the trouble?' they asked.

'I was carrying this wine across the ridge to sell in the village and stopped to cool off when these fellows asked if they could buy some,' the vendor said. 'I didn't let them have any. Then this merchant claimed my wine was drugged. Is he trying to be funny, or what?'

'*Pei!*' snorted the seven. 'We thought robbers had come, at least! So that's what all the row was about. Suppose he did say it – so what? We were just thinking of having some wine. If they're suspicious, sell a bucket to us. We'll drink it.'

'No, no! Nothing doing!' said the vendor.

'We didn't say anything against you, you stupid clod,' cried the seven. 'We'll give you the same price you'd get in the village. If you sell to us, what's the difference? You'll be doing a good deed, like handing out tea on a hot day, and quenching our thirst at the same time.'

'I don't mind selling you a bucket, but they said my wine is bad. Besides, I don't have any dipper.'

'You take things too seriously! What do you care what they said? We have our own dippers.'

Two of the date merchants brought out two coconut ladles from one of the wheel-barrows, while a third scooped up a big handful of dates. Then the seven gathered around the bucket and removed its cover. Ladling out the wine in turn, they drank, while munching the dates. Before long the bucket was empty.

'We haven't asked you the price yet,' said the seven.

'I never bargain,' the vendor asserted. 'Exactly five strings of cash per bucket – ten strings for the load.'

'Five strings you say, then five strings it shall be. But give us one free scoop out of the other bucket.'

'Can't be done. My prices are fixed!'

While one of the date merchants paid him the money, another opened the cover of the second bucket, ladled up some wine and started to drink it. The vendor hurried towards him, but the man walked quickly into the pine grove with the half consumed dipper of wine. As the vendor hastened after him, another merchant emerged from the grove with another ladle. He dipped this into the bucket and raised to his lips. The vendor rushed over, seized the ladle, and dumped its contents back into the bucket. Replacing the cover, he flung the ladle to the ground.

'You look like a proper man – why don't you act like one?' he fumed. 'Is that any way to behave?'

When the soldiers saw this, their throats felt even drier. All were longing for a drink. 'Put in a word for us, old grandpa,' one of them begged the chief steward. 'Those date merchants drank a bucket of his wine. Why shouldn't we buy the other and wet our throats? We're hot and thirsty and we haven't any other way. There's no place to get water on this ridge. Do us a favour, old grandpa!'

The old steward heard them out. He felt like having a drink himself. So he conferred with Yang Chih.

'Those date merchants have already finished a bucket of that vendor's wine. Only one bucket is left. Why not let them buy some wine and ward off heat stroke? There really isn't any place on this ridge to get water.'

Yang Chih thought to himself: 'I watched those birds finish off his first bucket, and drink half a ladleful from the second. The wine must be all right. I've been beating our porters for hours. Maybe

How the drug was put in the wine bucket while the soldiers were watching. A Ming illustration of Heroes of the Marshes

I ought to let them buy a few drinks.'

Aloud, he said: 'Since the chief steward suggests it, you rogues can have some wine. Then we'll march on.'

The soldiers chipped in and raised the price of a bucket. But the vendor refused them. 'I'm not selling, I'm not selling!' he said angrily. 'This wine is drugged!'

'Don't be like that, brother,' the soldiers said with placating smiles. 'Why rub it in?'

'I'm not selling,' said the vendor, 'so don't hang around!'

The date merchants intervened. 'Stupid oaf!' they berated him. 'What if that fellow said the wrong thing? You're much too serious. You've even tried to take it out on us. Anyhow, it has nothing to do with these porters. Sell them some wine and be done with it.'

'And give him a chance to cast suspicion on me for no reason at all?' the vendor demanded.

The date merchants pushed him aside and handed the bucket to the soldiers, who removed the cover. Having no ladles, they apologetically asked the merchants if they could borrow theirs.

'Have some dates, also, to go with your wine,' said the merchants. 'You're very kind!'

'No need to be polite. We're all travellers together. What do a hundred or so dates matter?'

The soldiers thanked them. The first two ladles of wine they presented to Yang Chih and the chief steward. Yang Chih refused, but the old man drank his. The next two ladlefuls were consumed by the two couriers. Then the soldiers swarmed around the bucket and imbibed heartily.

Yang Chih wavered. The soldiers showed no ill effects. Besides, the weather was hot and his throat was parched. Scooping up half a ladle of wine, he drank it while munching on a few dates.

'That date merchant drank a ladleful out of this bucket, so you had less wine,' the vendor said to the soldiers. 'You can pay me half a string of cash less.'

The soldiers gave him his money. The vendor took it, then, carrying his shoulder pole and empty buckets, he swung off down the ridge, again singing a folk-song.

Standing on the edge of the pine grove, the seven date merchants pointed at the fifteen men of the convoy and said: 'Down you go! Down you go!' The fifteen, weak in the knees and heavy in the head, stared at each other as, one by one, they sank to the ground. Then the seven merchants pushed the seven wheel-barrows out of the grove and dumped the dates. Placing the eleven loads of jewels and art objects into the barrows, they covered them over. 'Sorry to trouble you!' they called, and trundled off down the ridge.

Yang Chih, too weak to move, could only groan inwardly. The fifteen couldn't get up. They had only been able to goggle helplessly while the seven had loaded the barrows with the precious cargo. They were paralysed, bereft of speech.

Now I ask you—who were those seven men? None other than Chao Kai, Wu Yung, Kungsun Sheng, Liu Tang and the three Yuan brothers. And the wine vendor was Pai Sheng, nicknamed 'Rat Who Steals in Broad Daylight'. And how was the wine drugged? When the buckets were carried up the ridge, they contained pure wine. After the seven finished the first bucket, Liu Tang removed the cover from the second and deliberately drank half a ladleful so as to dull the others' suspicions. Next, inside the grove, Wu Yung poured the drug into the other ladle. Then he came out and spilled it into the wine while taking a 'free scoop'. As he pretended to drink, Pai Sheng grabbed the ladle and dumped the wine back in the bucket.

That was the ruse. Planned entirely by Wu Yung, it can be called 'Capturing the Birthday Gifts by Guile'.

Yang Chih had not drunk much, and he recovered quickly. Crawling to his feet, he could hardly stand. He looked at the other fourteen. Saliva was running from the corners of their mouths. None of them could move.

'You've made me lose the birthday gifts,' he muttered in angry despair. 'How can I even face the Governor Liang again? These convoy documents are worthless now!' He tore them up. 'I've become a man without a home or country. Where can I go? Better that I should die right here on this ridge!' Clutching his tunic, he staggered to the edge of the ridge and prepared to jump.

Truly: *Rains in the third month wash the fallen blossoms away, the last of willow tendrils the autumn frosts destroy.* Yang Chih sought death on Yellow Earth Ridge. What became of his life? Listen to our next instalment if you would know.

[What the next instalment reveals is that instead of committing suicide, Yang eventually goes on to join the heroes of the marshes. A man 'without home or country' has nowhere else to go.]

7 HOW THE DRAGON'S BACKBONE WAS INVENTED

It was not only gunpowder – the most familiar example – which was discovered in pre-industrial China long before it appeared in the West. China's early achievements in a wide field of science and technology have only lately begun to be fully appreciated. Here is the story of a third-century AD mechanical engineer, Ma Chun, who invented (or possibly developed from an earlier version) the 'dragon's backbone', a wooden chain-pump for raising water, which works on the conveyor-belt principle. Some of Ma's other inventions are also described, including the 'south-pointing chariot' which may have used some form of differential gear. Like some other inventors, Ma's gifts were 'all of the mind and not of the tongue', and he could not sell his technical skills very effectively. As the author of this article on Ma – a research fellow at the Chinese Academy of Sciences – points out, Ma's humble social background also lessened his chances of proper recognition.

The story of a 3rd-century AD mechanical engineer, China Reconstructs, *August 1964.*

One of the most ancient forms of Chinese irrigation equipment still in use today is the 'dragon's backbone' water lift. Though less efficient than modern electrified pumps which are now replacing it, the device does save a great deal of labour. Its widespread use has contributed immeasurably to agricultural production throughout more than 1700 years.

This water lift was only one of the inventions of Ma Chun, an outstanding mechanical engineer during the Three Kingdoms period (AD 220-280). Implements which he invented and improvements he made on the silk loom and farm tools played an important part in expanding the productive forces of his time. His construction of gear-operated devices occupies a glorious page in the annals of engineering in China.

Very little is known about Ma Chun's early life. He was born in a poor family in what is today Hsingping county in Shansi province. According to tradition, he virtually educated himself. He became a minor official in his native place, where he gained his first renown for improvements to the silk loom.

Although a loom capable of weaving brocades with intricate cloud, bird or animal patterns existed before his time, it worked so slowly that two months were needed to finish a single roll less than ten metres long. Ma Chun simplified the construction of the treadles that raised and lowered the warp threads to make the loom five times as fast as its predecessor.

Ma Chun's reputation as an inventor enabled him to take an official position in the capital of the Kingdom of Wei, Loyang, in present-day Honan province. There he noted that the rolling hills which rise up from the Lo River surrounding the city could be utilised for growing vegetables if water could be raised to irrigate them. The 'dragon's backbone' lift which he devised was probably similar in structure to one described in the thirteenth-century *Book of Agriculture* by Wang Chen, the earliest written account of such a device. It consisted of a trough with one end placed in the water. In it moved a series of flat pieces of wood, standing upright and closely fitting the trough. Through the centre of each were attached pieces of wood connected by movable joints spacing the boards at equal distances in what resembled a continuous circular belt. This ran over a large wheel at the top of the trough and a smaller one at the bottom. When the former was turned by hand, the boards moved upward in the manner of the buckets of a modern ladder dredge, raising water from the river to the fields.

Today in China one can see lifts of basically the same structure, except that they are turned by foot pedals, a later addition. The design has survived down to the present because of its extreme suitability to rural conditions. Requiring no metal, it could be built or repaired with simple tools using inexpensive and easily available materials. Because the lower end of the trough, being of wood, floats in the river, the buoyancy of the water bears up some of the weight of the water being lifted in the trough, thus lessening the work of the operator.

Ma Chun later became an adviser at the court of Wei Emperor Ming Ti, who reigned from 227 to 239. The following incident concerning him is related in the official annals, *History of the Three Kingdoms,* compiled by Chen Shou. One day the ministers were arguing about the marvellous chariot which the legendary emperor Huang Ti was said to have drawn with him through his battles. Once the pointer was set toward south at the beginning of a journey, it continued to point in that direction no matter how many turns the

33

経緯頗多巽君
好安排青綾不
歴歩去来々脈
脈歓欲乱巻く首脈
重四王言厂如絲
布付經緯才

Two examples of China's pre-industrial technology: above, 'throwing' the
silk onto a drum; opposite, a two-man version of the chain pump or 'dragon's
backbone'

emperor's own chariot made on winding mountain roads or in battle. One of Emperor Ming Ti's counsellors declared that there was no documentary proof that such a vehicle had ever been made. While the other officials agreed, Ma Chun remarked, 'I can see how such a chariot could be made.' When the others ridiculed him, Ma Chun offered to build one, and after securing the emperor's permission, did just that. Unfortunately neither this account nor any other tells the shape and structure of his creation.

South-pointing chariots are known to have been built repeatedly after Ma Chun's time, but the first extant description of the mechanism is of one made in 1027 by an engineer named Yen Hsu. Ma Chun's chariot was probably not identical, but we can assume that this later model followed the same principles. In addition to the body, Yen Hsu's chariot had five gears, two pulleys and two ground wheels. With one wheel as the pivot and its distance from the other wheel as the radius, if the chariot made a 90° turn in one direction, the gears moved the pointer 90° in the opposite direction to keep it in the original position.

As a guide for emperors on their travels, the south-pointer was not in itself of great importance. The lodestone had been known in China as early as the second century BC. During the Eastern Han period (AD 25-220), there were compasses made of a smooth bronze pan in which was placed a lodestone carved in the shape of a spoon, its handle indicating south. What is significant about the south-pointing chariot is that it shows Ma Chun was able to apply what was known about gears in an advanced way.

According to another incident related in the *History*, Emperor Ming Ti was presented with a miniature stage on which were placed many finely-carved figurines. Wishing them to move, he called in Ma Chun to improve upon them. The engineer made a prime mover turned by water which enabled the figures to travel about the stage as though alive. Through further use of gears he animated them so that the drummers, pipers and jugglers performed appropriate movements, archers drew back the strings of their bows, and acrobats climbed ropes and turned somersaults on horseback. Courtiers, fighting cocks, and workers hulling and grinding rice, went through many complicated motions.

Ma Chun could not have made these things had it not been for the economic and social conditions of his time. Many mechanisms based on the lever and gear had been in existence during the Han dynasty, which preceded his own. Among them were the water wheel for irrigation, water-powered blower used in smelting iron, the seismoscope and time-measuring instruments operated by water. The economy had begun to revive and grow as the peasant uprisings of the second century moved the feudal rulers to make some concessions to the people by reducing the tax burden and encouraging the opening of new land. Science and technology advanced to meet the needs of rising production. This economic base and the technical level already reached provided excellent conditions for Ma Chun's activity.

Unfortunately, the feudal rulers were not interested in the improvement of technology for production, so this creative engineer could not bring his talent into full play. Although in his lifetime Ma Chun was praised as 'a clever inventor known throughout the land' by Fu Hsuan (217-278), a contemporary writer and his friend, no official record of his birth or death was left to posterity. Even the references to him in the official annals are footnotes added a century later. Many of his inventions did not attract the interest of the court and were forgotten. As Fu Hsuan lamented, 'It is a pity that the state did not make full use of his talent.'

8 A GREAT CHINESE NAVIGATOR

China's achievements in nautical technology range from the invention of watertight compartments to the use of armour plating for the hulls of vessels of war. Both of these devices, and many others, were put into practice centuries before their discovery in the West. In the field of navigation we know that the magnetic compass was employed at sea at least a century and probably more before its Western counterpart. There were several periods of maritime exploration in imperial China; the last and most famous was the series of voyages to East Africa and the Indian Ocean which were conducted by the imperial eunuch Cheng Ho early in the Ming dynasty. Later a conservative reaction set in against these expeditions. Their logbooks and other records were destroyed, and it was made a capital offence to build ocean-going junks. But this episode of Cheng Ho's travels is one of quite a few exceptions to the commonly held rule that imperial China was 'isolated' from the rest of the world.

From an article in China Reconstructs, *July 1956*

Half a century before the world-renowned discoveries of Vasco da Gama, Columbus, Diaz and Magellan, the Chinese navigator Cheng Ho took huge fleets of hundreds of ships into the Indian Ocean. Between 1405 and 1433 he made seven voyages to the archipelagos of the South China Sea and the Indian, Arabian and East African coasts. The scale of these voyages was unparalleled in all previous world history. On three of the voyages, Cheng Ho's fleet carried 27,000 men. His cruises marked the most active period of China's maritime development.

China's seafaring tradition is very old. Her coastline stretches for 6000 miles, while thousands of islands dot her offshore waters. In the medieval period, such cities as Canton, Yangchow in Kiangsu province and Chuanchow in Fukien were centres of foreign trade, while Shanghai, Kanpu, Hangchow and Ningpo were rising seaports.

As early as the second century BC, according to our historical records, the emperor Wu-ti of the Han dynasty had sent a mission by sea to southern India. The compass, invented in China, helped navigation greatly and shipbuilding became highly developed. By the twelfth century, the geographical writer Chou Chu-fei was describing Chinese ships plying the southern seas as 'immense halls, with sails like clouds and rudders several *chang*[1] in length—each carrying hundreds of people and a year's supply of grain'.

In the fourteenth century, the Arab traveller Ibn Batuta wrote of a Chinese ocean vessel that could carry more than a thousand passengers. Its cabins were separated by thick bulkheads so that the ship could strike a rock and not sink. 'The master of the ship knew how to take his bearings by the stars at night and the sun in the day,' Ibn Batuta tells us, 'and on cloudy days he relied on the compass.' The Chinese also knew how to use the sounding lead to measure the depth of water.

Cheng Ho's voyages were a product of historical circumstances in the earlier period of the Ming dynasty (1368-1644). In 1281 during the preceding Yuan (Mongol) dynasty, the emperor Kublai Khan

[1]A *chang* is about 10 feet.

had sent a big fleet to invade Japan. This expedition met with complete disaster, comparable to that of the Spanish armada some three hundred years later. Afterwards China's power on the sea waned, while that of Japan grew. By the beginning of the Ming dynasty, Japanese raiders were landing regularly on the shores of Shantung and other provinces. China had to look to the rebuilding of her maritime strength.

There was another contributing circumstance. From 1366 to 1405, contemporaneously with the first decades of Ming rule in China, the empire of the Turco-Mongol conqueror Tamerlane threatened her western borders. Then, and for many years later, China's overland trade with Western Asia and India was blocked. This turned Chinese attention to the expansion of seaborne trade – much as the later fall of Constantinople to the Turks stimulated navigation in Europe.

Facing such situations on both land and sea, the first Ming emperor, Hung Wu (1368-99), prepared to develop a navy as an instrument of trade and national power. He set up a shipyard, planted hundreds of thousands of varnish and tung trees on Purple Mountain at his capital of Nanking, and founded a foreign language institute to train interpreters. He also sent envoys to Central Asia to acquaint themselves with conditions in Tamerlane's dominions, to Srivijaya (now Palembang) in Sumatra, and Borneo and Cola in Southern India, to make diplomatic and commercial contacts. By the accession of the third Ming emperor, Yung Lo, in 1403, China's national economy had more than recovered from the ravages of Mongol rule and the subsequent long years of internal war. The country was orderly and growing richer. The development of work-shop manufacture and home trade brought a demand for foreign markets. Yung Lo, who had seized the throne from his nephew and was personally unpopular, considered it necessary to raise his prestige by some spectacular undertaking.

The Ming Dynastic History tells us that the reasons for Cheng Ho's expeditions were that the emperor 'suspected that Hui Ti (the nephew whom he had deposed) had escaped abroad, and wanted to track him down, also the emperor wanted to show his military strength to foreign countries'. It is probable that the first motive was only a pretext, and the second is certainly not a complete state-ment, because it makes no mention of trade. Actually, the advance of China's productive economy and techniques, as well as her domestic political situation, combined to form a background for the voyages.

What about Cheng Ho himself, and why was he chosen to head

The eunuch Cheng Ho on his flagship. From a popular Ming novel based on his voyages

the huge fleets that were built? A native of Kunyang in Yunnan province, Cheng Ho came of a household of the Semur national minority, Muslim in faith. His surname at birth was Ma, a very common one among Mohammedans in China. His grandfather's given name was Bayan, his father's Haji, and they had both been pilgrims to Mecca. The family probably originated in Central Asia and came to Yunnan with the Mongol conquest. From the tombstone he erected for his father in Yunnan in 1405, which still stands near the Kunyang city gate, we know that Cheng Ho was the younger of two sons and had four sisters. In 1382 the Ming armies defeated the Mongols in Yunnan, one of their last strongholds. Cheng Ho, still a child, was among the captives brought back to Nanking. There he was made a eunuch and assigned to the service of the Prince of Yen, who later became the emperor Yung Lo. It was the emperor who gave him his new surname, Cheng.

The historical records say that Cheng Ho was a tall, burly man with 'clear-cut features and long ear-lobes; a stride like a tiger's and a voice clear and vibrant'. He is described as having been sharp and quick-witted in argument, yet diligent, modest and well-liked by all his acquaintances. In his youth, he fought in the Prince of Yen's campaign to seize the throne and, distinguishing himself, became a confidant of the emperor. The eunuchs, who had given much help to this campaign, became an influential group in the new court. Since Cheng Ho's father and grandfather had been as far as Mecca, he had some knowledge of foreign lands. This, with his abilities and his closeness to the ruler, made him a natural choice as envoy to the 'western seas' – an expression then used to denote places west of Malacca.

Cheng Ho set out in 1405. His seven voyages extended over about thirty years. With the exception of six years between the last two, when he was garrison commander of Nanking, he spent most of that time at sea. . . .

In the first voyage (1405-7), Cheng Ho touched on Champa on the coast of present-day Indo-China, then went on to Java, Malacca, Palembang in Sumatra, and Calicut. The second (1407-9) followed the same route as far as Malacca, then took in Ceylon, Calicut, Quilan and Cochin, stopping in Siam on the return trip. The third (1409-11) was roughly the same as the second – with reason to believe that some ships went to the Nicobar Islands.

It was on the fourth voyage (1413-15) that the fleet first went beyond Calicut, sailing on to the Maldive Islands and Ormuz on the

Persian Gulf. The fifth (1417–19) was still more far-ranging, going on from Ormuz to Aden, and thence to Mogadishu, Brava and Jobo on the Somali Coast of East Africa. The sixth (1421-2) ended once more. at Ormuz, but is the first one known definitely to have included Bengal, though it is probable that previous visits to Bengal had been made.

On the seventh and last voyage (1430-33), Ceylon was revisited. From Ormuz the ships went to the Arabian coast, with some members of the expedition going to Mecca. There is reason to believe, however, that this was not the first visit to the Muslim goal of pilgrimage.

All Cheng Ho's voyages were organised on a gigantic scale. On the second, fourth and seventh, the crews and other personnel numbered over 27,000 in each case. They included troops, sailors, ship repairmen, victuallers, scribes, geomancers and physicians. The number of physicians on the fourth voyage was 180, averaging about one to every 150 persons on the expedition. For purposes of negotiation, Cheng Ho found it was to his advantage to take along a Muslim of position. Before setting out on his fourth voyage, he went personally to Sian to invite Hassan, the Imam of the Ching Chin Mosque there, to sail in his retinue. On the fifth voyage, the Buddhist monk Hui Sheng accompanied him 'for official business in the western seas'.

Most of Cheng Ho's ships were built by the imperial yards at Dragon River Pass, a few miles up the Yangtze from Nanking, where hundreds of shipwrights had been brought from coastal and river provinces. Others were constructed in Fukien province, and Taichang in Kiangsu. The big vessels, according to the Ming Dynastic History, were 44.4 *chang* (over 600 feet) long with a beam of over 250 feet. Those of medium size were 500 feet long with a beam of some 200 feet. All had names and numbers as in a modern navy. On the fourth voyage there were 63 vessels, with an average of 430 persons on board each. . . .

In those days, trade between China and the 'western seas' was brisk. The Chinese ships carried such goods as the famed Ming blue-and-white porcelains; silk fabrics including satin, brocade and pongee; cottons including prints and the durable, firm-textured brownish-yellow cloth known as Nankeen because it was originally woven in Nanking; gold and silver; iron and copper ware; pepper, grain and musk. These were exchanged for spices, dye-stuffs, medicinal herbs and products, precious stones and pearls, rhinoceros horn, ivory, peacock feathers and tropical animals. . . .

On each voyage the fleet anchored at Malacca, then the cross-roads of South Sea navigation, where it separated into groups. At Malacca, we learn, 'warehouses were built to store money and provisions, and home-bound ships assembled to sort out their foreign goods and wait for the south wind in mid-March to take them back (to China)'. The Malacca base, which was probably set up during the first voyage, was a great help to Cheng Ho's subsequent enterprises.

The Chinese mariners recorded many interesting facts about the countries they visited. In Champa, Java and Sumatra they found many of their fellow-countrymen, merchants and artisans who had migrated from the coastal provinces, especially Kwangtung, as early as Tang times (AD 618-907). In Java, wrote Ma Huan, besides the indigenous population and the Chinese there were many merchants from Persia and the Arab lands. In Bengal, Aden and other places, local kings and princes came to the coast themselves to welcome the fleet. In Ceylon, its emissaries visited a Buddhist monastery, where they made offerings of gold and silver, streamers of cloth-of-gold, censers, vases, lanterns and candles. They also erected a stone tablet there, and it is proof of the accuracy of their records that the tablet was found in 1911.

The culture of India, Persia and Arabia impressed them deeply. Ma Huan wrote of the music he heard at Calicut: 'Songs were accompanied by musical instruments made of gourds with strings of red copper wire, and the sound and rhythm was pleasant to the ear.' He mentioned that the ruler of Calicut presented the visitors with a sash made of 50 ounces of pure gold 'reeled into hair-fine threads, interlaced, and studded with large pearls and precious stones of every hue'. He gave high praise to the skill of the physicians, geomancers and artisans of Bengal and Ormuz, the acrobats of Persia and the jewellers of Aden. Both he and Ma Huan gave detailed descriptions of the Ka'aba Mosque in Mecca, with its majestic gates and pillars. Also visited was the tomb of Mohammed at Medina.

Chinese navigation did not develop after Cheng Ho. The land-lord-scholar officials of subsequent reigns condemned his expeditions as expensive and useless – and even burned his logs and reports in the national archives, so that we are left only with general descriptions and the memoirs of participants.

Nonetheless the voyages were a brilliant page in the history of China's maritime enterprise and foreign relations. After them, envoys of many countries in the 'western seas' came to the Ming court, bringing goods for trade. Widening markets abroad stimulated workshop production at home. More and more Chinese went to Southeast Asia for business and settlement. The economic and cultural intercourse that developed benefitted both sides.

Inside China, stories of the exploits of 'the Eunuch San Pao', as Cheng Ho was officially known, gained wide currency among the people. At the end of the Ming dynasty, a play about them was performed at court. Lo Mou-teng, in 1597, wrote a 100-chapter novel entitled *The Western Sea Cruises of Eunuch San Pao*, which is still read today.

It is as San Pao that Cheng Ho is also remembered in many of the countries he visited. In Malacca, there is still a San Pao Town and San Pao Well. In Java there are the San Pao Mound at Semarang, the San Pao Cave and San Pao Temple.

The great navigator did much for trade between China and countries of Asia and Africa, and for their mutual knowledge. Today, when their contacts are being restored on a new basis, it is fit that we remember his contribution.

MODERN CHINA
A Century of Struggle

9 A LETTER TO QUEEN VICTORIA

In the textbooks it is usually called the First Anglo-Chinese War, but for most people and especially for the Chinese it has always been the Opium War (1839-42). Opium, as one British Viceroy of India described it, 'is a pernicious article of luxury, which ought not to be permitted but for the purposes of foreign commerce'. The sale of Indian opium to the Chinese, mostly by British traders, made a healthy contribution to Indian revenues while it also financed the purchase of Chinese silks and teas for the British market. The sale and use of opium was prohibited by imperial decree from Peking but with little success. In 1839 the emperor appointed a special commissioner, Lin Tse-hsu, to enforce the prohibition of opium at Canton – the one port which foreigners were traditionally allowed to use. Lin on his arrival drafted a letter to Queen Victoria, unable to believe that she or her ministers knew of this traffic being conducted by her subjects. The letter apparently was never sent. Lin confiscated the traders' opium and burnt it publicly; to the British this was sufficient grounds for war.

Translated by Arthur Waley in The Opium War through Chinese Eyes

The Way of Heaven is fairness to all; it does not suffer us to harm others in order to benefit ourselves. Men are alike in this all the world over: that they cherish life and hate what endangers life. Your country lies twenty thousand leagues away; but for all that the Way of Heaven holds good for you as for us, and your instincts are not different from ours; for nowhere are there men so blind as not to distinguish between what brings life and what brings death, between what brings profit and what does harm. Our Heavenly Court treats all within the Four Seas as one great family; the goodness of our great Emperor is like Heaven, that covers all things. There is no region so wild or so remote that he does not cherish and tend it.

Canton at the time of the Opium War. Foreign factories line the bank of the Pearl River

Ever since the port of Canton was first opened, trade has flourished. For some hundred and twenty or thirty years the natives of the place have enjoyed peaceful and profitable relations with the ships that come from abroad. Rhubarb, tea, silk are all valuable products of ours, without which foreigners could not live. The Heavenly Court, extending its benevolence to all alike, allows these things to be sold and carried away across the sea, not grudging them even to remote domains, its bounty matching the bounty of Heaven and Earth.

But there is a class of evil foreigner that makes opium and brings it for sale, tempting fools to destroy themselves, merely in order to reap profit. Formerly the number of opium smokers was small; but now the vice has spread far and wide and the poison penetrated deeper and deeper. If there are some foolish people who yield to this craving to their own detriment, it is they who have brought upon themselves their own ruin, and in a country so populous and flourishing, we can well do without them. But our great, unified Manchu Empire regards itself as responsible for the habits and morals of its subjects and cannot rest content to see any of them become victims to a deadly poison. For this reason we have decided to inflict very severe penalties on opium dealers and opium smokers, in order to put a stop for ever to the propagation of this vice. It appears that this poisonous article is manufactured by certain devilish persons in places subject to your rule. It is not, of course, either made or sold at your bidding, nor do all the countries you rule produce it, but only certain of them. I am told that in your own country opium smoking is forbidden under severe penalties. This means that you are aware of how harmful it is. But better than to forbid the smoking of it would be to forbid the sale of it and, better still, to forbid the production of it, which is the only way of cleansing the contamination at its source. So long as you do not take it yourselves, but continue to make it and tempt the people of China to buy it, you will be showing yourselves careful of your own lives, but careless of the lives of other people, indifferent in your greed for gain to the harm you do to others; such conduct is repugnant to human feeling and at variance with the Way of Heaven. Our Heavenly Court's resounding might, redoubtable to its own subjects and foreigners alike, could at any moment control their fate; but in its compassion and generosity it makes a practice of giving due warning before it strikes. Your Majesty has not before been thus officially notified, and you may plead ignorance of the severity of our laws. But I now give my assurance that we mean to cut

THE CHINESE OPIUM-SMOKER.

No. 6.

It is easy to imagine the feelings of the unfortunate wife, who, seeing the misery and wretchedness wrought in her once comfortable home, determines to destroy the whole of the smoking apparatus. The tray and lamp are dashed upon the floor, a few more moments will see the destruction of the pipe itself; but the noise has reached the ears of her lord, who rushes in, and, forgetful of all the teachings of his great master, Confucius, proceeds to belabour her with the bamboo stick he has seized for the purpose, in spite of the cries of their unfortunate child. The entrance of an old and faithful retainer alone prevents him from inflicting serious injury.

Not everyone supported the opium trade – a page from a late Victorian anti-opium tract with Chinese-style illustrations

off this harmful drug for ever. What it is here forbidden to consume, your dependencies must be forbidden to manufacture, and what has already been manufactured Your Majesty must immediately search out and throw it to the bottom of the sea, and never allow such a poison to exist in Heaven or on earth. When that is done, not only will the Chinese be rid of this evil, but your people too will be safe. For so long as your subjects make opium, who knows but they will not sooner or later take to smoking it; so that an embargo on the making of it may very well be a safeguard for them, too. Both nations will enjoy the blessing of a peaceful existence, yours on its side having made clear its sincerity by respectful obedience to our commands. You will be showing that you understand the principles of Heaven, and calamities will be not sent down on you from above; you will be acting in accordance with decent feeling, which may also well influence the course of nature in your favour.

The laws against the consumption of opium are now so strict in China that if you continue to make it, you will find that no one buys it and no more fortunes will be made. Rather than waste your efforts on a hopeless endeavour, would it not be better to devise some other form of trade? All opium discovered in China is being cast into burning oil and destroyed. Any foreign ships that in the future arrive with opium on board, will be set on fire too, and any other goods that they are carrying will inevitably be burnt along with the opium. You will then not only fail to make any profit out of us, but ruin yourselves into the bargain. Intending to harm others, you will be the first to be harmed. Our Heavenly Court would not have won the allegiance of innumerable lands did it not wield superhuman power. Do not say you have not been warned in time. On receiving this, Your Majesty will be so good as to report to me immediately on the steps that have been taken at each of your ports.

10 THE IMPERIALISTS, THE PEOPLE AND THE MANDARINS

The Treaty of Nanking, imposed upon the Chinese at the end of the Opium War, gave the British the right to trade and reside at five ports, including that of Canton to which trade had previously been confined. (Later Treaties signed by France and the United States gave other foreigners the same privileges.) In Canton, where because of the city's greater experience of Western behaviour popular feeling against the British ran high, the foreigners were confined to their original settlement and kept outside the city walls. The wording of the Treaty itself provided some legal justification for this. If given the chance to enter the city, the foreign merchants would probably have stayed outside, but the Chinese refusal was regarded as an intolerable 'arrogance'. This was one of the major issues leading to the second War of 1856-61, which began with the British capture of Canton on the pretext of a trivial incident. This account of the struggle for Canton in the 1840s, written by the communist historian Hu Sheng, lays stress on the vigour of the people's resistance and on the weakness of their officials' response. Hu's interpretation is generally borne out by documents and eye-witness reports of the time. Not only the 'English robbers' but the 'cannibal mandarins' were denounced in wall-posters put up by the Canton 'mob' (which is how the people were usually described in the dispatches of both Chinese and British officials). And anti-foreign feeling would later turn into anti-Manchu rebellion.

From Imperialism and Chinese Politics, *Peking 1955*

The foreign powers, unable to send diplomatic representatives to Peking, had so far established contact and negotiated only with the officials at the specified treaty ports. The Manchu Government entrusted the direction of foreign affairs of the empire to the viceroy of Kwangtung and Kwangsi, who had his headquarters at Canton. Thus Canton became the centre of China's foreign relations. No sooner had the Nanking Treaty been signed than the British demanded the opening of Canton and the right of entry into the city. The treaty, however, contained no reference to the British entry into the city. The population of Canton raised protest after protest against the British demands; placards in red and white were pasted up in every street, attacking the officials who had compromised with the British and appealing to both the gentry and the people to get ready to repulse the British should they force their way in. The dispute over the British entry into the city of Canton lasted more than ten years. Not until the Second Opium War were the British able to fight their way into Canton. The struggle waged by

德澤及民

A local magistrate's court. Beating with sticks was the lightest form of punishment. 'Virtue extends to the people', reads the inscription

the people in Canton bears out the fact that, during the Opium War, it was the Manchu rulers, and not the people, who had submitted. The fact that the people, with the degree of political consciousness they possessed at the time, had put up resolute resistance, not only alarmed the aggressors but greatly worried the Manchu rulers. Thus in the ten-year-old dispute over the British entry into the city of Canton we may see clearly the changes which took place in the relationships between the officials, the people and the foreigners (the autocratic rulers, the common people and the aggressive forces) after the Opium War.

In December 1842, four months after the signing of the Treaty of Nanking, an incident occurred in Canton in which English sailors were involved in a fight with the Chinese. Some foreign business houses were burned down. Reporting this incident to the court, Chi Kung, Viceroy of Kwangtung and Kwangsi, wrote:

After the ships of the British barbarians returned to Hong-kong from Fukien and Chekiang, the foreigners became more and more insolent. There are many cases in which sailors who live in the 13 foreign hongs [factories] maltreated the common people, robbed shops when drunk and insulted women who passed by. The local officials took measures to suppress these disturbances and because of this they did not develop into serious incidents. However, the population, filled with resentment, was all for settling accounts with the foreign barbarians. On the 23rd day of the 10th moon, someone, acting in the name of the 'Ming Lun Tang', pasted up placards, denouncing the crimes of the foreigners and threatening retaliatory action. . . . On the afternoon of the 6th day of the 11th moon (7 December 1842), a British sailor bought fruit from a Chinese in the vicinity of the 13 foreign hongs but refused to pay. The vendor asked him to pay and in reply the sailor stabbed and wounded him. This was witnessed by a crowd of people who were greatly incensed by the outrage. Realising he was in the wrong, the sailor ran away to the tall building where he lived and bolted the gate. The crowd pursued him home. Excitement grew as the people surrounding the building shouted at the foreigners. The latter flung stones at the crowd from the upper storey of the building. On being informed of this incident, we at once instructed the local officials to go to the spot to investigate and to restore order. By night the crowd had gradually dispersed. Suddenly the building went up in flames. . . . Since then, this spot has been watched and guarded day and night by officers and men and it has been quiet since the 7th. Realising that they had roused the ire of the local populace, the foreigners became very frightened. But when the officials saw to their safety, the foreigners calmed down and expressed gratitude to the authorities.

Judging from this report, the situation was very clear: the people had every reason to rise against foreigners, and the officials, occupied as they were with appeasing the foreigners, had certainly failed in their duty to protect the people.

In 1843 Kiying, who had signed the Treaty of Nanking, was sent to Kwangtung as imperial commissioner. As soon as he arrived he charged 'the local riff-raff' with engineering all the anti-foreign outbursts. He added: 'Mutual suspicions and mistrusts have poisoned the relations between the people and the foreigners and if these are not handled properly untoward incidents will again occur.' It is clear that he was trying to present the officials as being superior both to the people and the foreigners and at the same time as neutrals in the disputes between them. In fact, what the officials did was to suppress the people and to appease the foreigners. It was not surprising therefore that the people felt very strongly about this situation. According to an Englishman, many of the placards appearing in the streets of Canton strongly attacked the local authorities. One placard, for instance, read in part:

Our cannibal mandarins have hitherto been the accomplices of the English robbers in all the acts that the latter have committed against order and justice. . . . In the fifth moon of the present year, many Chinese have been slain by foreigners; their bodies have been flung into the river, and buried in the bellies of fishes; but our high authorities have treated these affairs as though they have never heard of them; they have looked upon these foreign devils as though they were gods; they have despised the Chinese as though they had the flesh of dogs; and have not valued the life of men more than the hair which is shorn from the head. They persist in keeping the throne in ignorance of what is passing, and in neglecting to treat this affair with the importance it deserves. Thousands of people are filled with grief and anger; sorrow has penetrated the marrow of their bones, and their sole consolation is to express their woes in the public assemblies.

Thus, Tsao Lu-tai, Supervising Censor of Hukuang (Hupeh and Hunan), was not wrong when he wrote in a memorial to the throne in 1846: 'The deep cleavage between the officials and the people has existed for quite a long time. . . . The hostility of the people of Canton towards foreigners means nothing less than the hostility of the people towards the local officials.'

In January 1846 Kiying, Viceroy of Kwangtung and Kwangsi, bowed to the British and proclaimed the city of Canton open to foreigners. The people at once rose in revolt against this decision. The office of the prefect was burned down by the masses who opposed the officials currying favour with the foreigners. For a time, confusion reigned in Canton. And because of popular opposition, the question of the opening of Canton was deferred.

In these circumstances, the British would have had to cope with a lot of trouble if they had tried to force their way into Canton. They thought it best to do nothing but watch warily. It was precisely because of this that they resented all the more bitterly the inability of the Manchu officials to suppress the people's anti-foreign sentiments so as to ensure 'the implementation of the treaty obligations'. In 1847 British gunboats forced their way into the Pearl River and, making use of threats, compelled Kiying to agree to open the city of Canton in two years' time. Reporting this to the emperor, Kiying wrote: 'During the past few years I have done everything possible to mediate in the dispute between the people and the foreigners, yet, this has not prevented the latest incident. I am deeply ashamed of myself.' Kiying, throughout, had regarded the dispute as one concerning only the people and the foreigners, with the officials playing the role of mediators between them.

After the Opium War, the Manchu authorities were still ignorant of the size of the foreigners' appetite. Whenever the foreigners used threats, they submitted to the dictates of the foreign powers and flouted the opinion of the people. But when the foreigners appeared more or less 'appeased' and the feeling of the people was running high they hesitated about doing what the foreign powers wanted them to do, calculating that it was in their own interests to heed a little the voice of the people.

In view of the unmistakable mood of the people of Canton, and seeing that the British were wavering on the question of the opening of the city of Canton and had actually agreed to put it off for another two years, the Manchu authorities felt that, despite their position of mediators between the people and the foreigners, they would be well advised to lean a little more towards the people. Therefore, when in 1849 the British demanded from the Manchu authorities to fulfil the promise about opening the city of Canton, Hsu Kuang-chin, who had succeeded Kiying as Viceroy of Kwangtung and Kwangsi, refused to comply with the demand and lectured the British in the following terms: 'The people are the pillars of the state and since the people have refused to open the city of Canton, the emperor is in no mood to force them to do so just to please foreigners.'

As a matter of fact, the people of Canton, irrespective of the attitude the authorities might assume in this matter, had orgnised

TO19317

themselves into a force of more than one hundred thousand men, holding themselves in readiness to resist. In these circumstances, Hsu Kuang-chin considered it well advised to adopt a strong policy towards the foreigners, knowing well that to act otherwise would bring the weight of the one hundred thousand men upon his own head.

Explaining to the emperor the reason for his policy, Hsu wrote:

To parry off the British demand would not necessarily precipitate incidents (that is to say, it was still possible to hold the British off with promise and delaying tactics). On the contrary, acquiescence in their demands would certainly lead to a clash of arms (that is to say, the people would have taken arms to repel the aggressor). Moreover, if we deny them entry into the city, thus bringing on untoward incidents, the people will rise and we may depend on their support (that is to say, the strength of the people can be brought into play). If, however, we acquiesce in the foreigners' demand and allow them to enter the city, the people will rise and this will lead to internal and external disturbances (that is to say, the people would rise against the government).

Thus, Hsu Kuang-chin's policy was based on the same motives as that of Kiying: both tried to follow a course of action calculated to ward off the most imminent danger, at the given time, to the interests of the Manchu rulers. The strong policy followed by Hsu Kuang-chin had nothing in common with the stand taken by the people. The officials posed as mediators between the people and the foreigners, but this political manoeuvre failed to eliminate the contradictions between the broad masses of the people and the rulers.

11 AN ENGLISHMAN'S JUDICIOUS OPINION ON WAR WITH CHINA

For once we shall use an extract from a non-Chinese source to illustrate (certainly against the writer's intention) the Chinese point of view. Robert Swinhoe of Her Majesty's Consular Service was interpreter to General Sir Hope Grant, the commander of the British forces which together with the French thrust their way into Peking in 1860. The story of the war is a confused one; each side accused the other of bad faith and treachery. But the essential issue was Britain's determination to gain diplomatic access to Peking and commercial access to more Chinese ports (the French were more interested in privileges for their missionaries), and China's determination to fend off the foreigners. Swinhoe like most of his countrymen had no doubt that foreign trade plus Christianity would be good business for the Chinese as well as for the traders. Note in particular his reference to the Taiping Rebellion which had challenged Manchu rule in Central China for more than ten years – Britain's attitude towards the rebels, he argues, should depend upon 'the good conduct they show towards the promotion of trade'. Earlier in his narrative, Swinhoe describes a looting episode in the countryside near Tientsin. The peasants who suffered from it had, he claims, 'none to blame but their own pig-headed obstinacy in not having removed, at the first arrival of the [British] ships, which they could plainly see from the land, all the goods and chattels that they cared to preserve'. This, for the Chinese, is the authentic voice of imperialism to which they listened in one form or another for a century of their modern history.

From Swinhoe's Narrative of the North China Campaign

It remains with our civil authorities now mildly to insist on the performance of what our arms have so ably won. To the few ports we before had permission to resort to, we now have an accession of several others, which in the course of a few years are likely to prove vastly greater emporiums of trade; and while additional wealth is wafted thence to the shores of Great Britain, we trust, in return, that Christianity, with her civilising influences, may gradually flow in, and, taking firm hold on China's millions, lead them to bless the scourge of war that for a few short months ravaged their lands, and, in spite of their preconceived hostility to foreign opinions, insisted on right of access being granted to foreign nations. The opening of Neuchwang lays patent to our mart free competition with encroaching Russia. Tang-chow and Tien-tsin put us in possession of the high roads of commerce to the capital. Swatow throws open a fine river bordering the provinces of Canton and Fuhkeen; and promising fields are offered to us in the large and little-known islands of Hainan and Formosa. The much-desired admission to the heart of China is also now secured by the ports opened to our commerce on its shores, whence access is procured to the vast lands

Two views of the Western allies' landing, August 1860. Above, 'The ground ... was literally strewn with the enemy's dead and wounded' – engraved by an artist with the British forces. Below, a Chinese impression of the storming of the Taku Forts

where the best teas and silks are manufactured. The great obstacle there, however, is the devastating inroads of the rebels, who, to the disappointment of all interested in their movements, have lately well proved that plunder is their object and luxury their god. But they have very properly been taught by the late repulse they received at Shanghai, from the hands of the Allies, that their existence depends on the good conduct they show towards the promotion of trade. Rebellion, such as this, which amounts to little else than brigandism, is an event always to be dreaded in whatever country; but it is not for me to point out the course that should be pursued, whether of strict neutrality or of interference on the imperialist [Manchu Government's] side. It is true that the energy of China is at present much shaken; but, as in former years she has ridden through similar storms, if her history speak true, it is not improbable she may yet regain strength, and in one mighty effort quench this glowing spark that has for years been slowly consuming her vitals. The field is now open for us, and it is our course to 'go in and win'. By upholding firmly the character and honour of our country, and at once resenting any show of enmity, we may long continue to maintain friendly relations on a satisfactory footing, and gradually develop the vast resources of this country. The footing we have now gained is mainly due to the success of the late expedition, which, thanks to the exertions of all the departments concerned, was enabled to supply, notwithstanding the vast distance travelled, the most complete army, perfect in all its branches, that has ever yet taken the field; and though every Englishman naturally grumbles at the expense incurred, yet he cannot help feeling gratification at its signal success, more especially when he surveys the large tract of country it has thrown open to our enterprise, and from which great advantages are likely to be derived.

12 A REPORT ON THE COOLIE TRADE

In the Treaty imposed on China after the war of 1860 one clause stipulated that all Chinese were 'at perfect liberty' to enter into service 'in the British colonies and other parts beyond sea'. This amounted to the legalisation of the Chinese coolie trade, by which cheap Chinese labour was supplied to the rubber and tin plantations of Java and the Straits Settlements, the sugar plantations of Cuba and the West Indies, the gold mines and railroads of California. Emigration brokers in the Chinese treaty ports grew rich on the trade; so did the foreign owners who transported the coolies, often in slave-ship conditions. In 1866 China sought to negotiate an agreement with Britain and France which would provide all Chinese emigrants with a five-year contract and the right to a free passage home. This was rejected on the grounds of expense. Even allowing for a 20-per-cent mortality rate on the job, it was argued in London, the free passage entitlement meant that Chinese coolies would cost twice as much as Indian coolies. The traffic continued with little regulation. In 1873 the Chinese Government, alarmed at the small proportion of emigrants returning from Cuba after their terms of service, sent a three-man commission 'to ascertain the conditions of Chinese coolies in Cuba'. A year later the commission reported back in judicial but horrified terms:

From the Report of the Cuba Commission

. . . All investigations of Chinese were conducted verbally and in person by ourselves. The depositions and petitions show that eight-tenths of the entire number declared that they had been kidnapped or decoyed; that the mortality during the voyage from wounds caused by blows, suicide and sickness proves to have exceeded ten per cent; that on arrival at Havana they were sold into slavery – a small proportion being disposed of to families and shops, whilst the large majority became the property of sugar planters; that the cruelty displayed even towards those of the former class is great, and that it assumes in the case of those of the latter, proportions that are unendurable. The labour, too, on the plantations is shown to be excessively severe, and the food to be insufficient; the hours of labour are too long, and the chastisements by rods, whips, chains, stocks, &c., &c., productive of suffering and injury. During the past years a large number have been killed by blows, have died from the effects of wounds and have hanged themselves, cut their throats, poisoned themselves with opium, and thrown themselves into wells and sugar cauldrons. It was also possible to verify by personal inspection wounds inflicted upon others, the fractured and

Missionaries, allowed to enter China by the 1860 Treaties, wearing 'native dress' with pigtails. The text says that all who believe shall have everlasting life

maimed limbs, blindness, the heads full of sores, the teeth struck out, the ears mutilated, and the skin and flesh lacerated, proofs of cruelty patent to the eyes of all.

On the termination of the contracts the employers, in most cases, withhold the certificates of completion, and insist on renewal of engagements, which may extend to even more than ten years, and during which the same system of cruelty is adhered to; whilst if the Chinese refuse to assent, they are taken to the depots, whence in chains, and watched by guards, they are forced to repair roads, receiving no compensation for their labour, undergoing a treatment exactly similar to that of criminals in jail. Afterwards they are compelled to again enter the service of an employer, and sign a contract, on the completion of which they are once more taken to the depots; and as this process is constantly repeated, a return home, and an attempt to gain a livelihood independently, become impossible.

Moreover, since the 2nd moon of the 11th year of Hienfêng [March-April 1861] the issue of Letters of Domicile and Cedulas has ceased, rendering liability to arrest universal, whilst those possessing these papers are constantly, be it on the street or in their own houses, called upon to produce them for inspection, or are even exposed to their being taken away, or torn up, and to themselves being carried away to the endless misery of a depot. Of all these facts the depositions and petitions furnish detailed evidence. . . .

The majority of the Chinese Coolies in Cuba sailed from Macao, Amoy, Swatow and Canton. They were mainly decoyed abroad, not legitimately induced to emigrate. . . . The petition of Liu A-shou and four others states, 'we were decoyed to the Macao barracoons, and though not inspected by any Portuguese officials, were, after the evening meal – our queues having been tied together, and guarded by foreign soldiers armed with firearms – forced to embark, whilst no one heeded the cries for aid which we uttered on the way.'[1] The petition of Chang Ting-chia and 127 others states, 'we were decoyed to and sold at Havana, by vicious men.' The petition of Cheng A-mou and eighty-nine others states, 'we were induced to proceed to Macao by offers of employment abroad at high wages, and through being told that the eight foreign years specified in the contracts were equivalent to only four Chinese, and that at the

[1]A barracoon is any kind of enclosure into which people can be herded. The queue was the pigtail which Chinese were forced to wear by the Manchu emperors.

termination of the latter period we would be free. We observed also on the signboards of the foreign buildings the words 'agencies for the engagement of labourers', and believed that they truthfully described the nature of the establishments, little expecting that having once entered the latter, exit would be denied us; and when on arrival at Havana, we were exposed for sale and subjected to appraisement in a most ruthless manner, it became evident that we were not to be engaged as labourers, but to be sold as slaves.'

Again it is gathered from the 1176 depositions which have been recorded that of those who sailed from Macao Wen Ch'ang-t'ai and sixty-five others were kidnapped, that Tseng Erh-ch'i and 689 others were decoyed, that Liu A-jui and fifty others were entrapped into signing contracts in the belief that they were merely doing so in the place of others temporarily absent, that Huang A-mu and ninety-three others were the victims of various snares tendered to them after they had gambled and lost, and that Ch'en A-chi and sixty-five others emigrated voluntarily. . . .

Yen A-huan and one other likewise depose, that when being sold their clothes were removed, and their persons examined in order to ascertain whether they possessed strength, in the manner practised when oxen or horses are being bought. Chang A-hsi and one other depose, that when being sold their clothes were removed and their persons were felt and examined, just as is done in country districts when an ox is being bought. Chiang San deposes, 'in the Havana barracoon, for refusing to permit the removal of my queue, I was beaten almost to death'. Li A-ling deposes, 'it is the custom when coolies are being sold to remove their clothing to enable the buyer to effect a thorough examination of the person' . . .

The petition of Li Chao-ch'un and 165 others states, 'ninety per-cent are disposed of to the sugar plantations. There the owners rely upon the administrator for the production of a large crop of sugar, and the administrator looks to the overseers for the exaction of the greatest possible amount of labour. They all think only of the profit to be gained and are indifferent as to our lives. It matters not whether the workmen are miserable or contented, whether they starve or have enough to eat, whether they live or die. The administrator who gives only four unripe bananas as a meal, is considered an able servant, and if he gives only three he is regarded as still more efficient. The administrator who forces the Chinese to work twenty hours out of the twenty-four is a man of capacity, if he extorts twenty-one his qualities are of a still higher order, but he may strike, or flog, or chain us, as his fancy suggests to him. If we complain of sickness we are beaten and starved; if we work slowly dogs are urged after us to bite us. Those of us who are employed on farms or coffee estates, in sugar warehouses and brick-kilns, on railways and in baker, cigar, shoe, hat and other shops, are in each of these places of service, ill treated, flogged, confined in stocks and in jail, and tortured in every way as on the plantations.' The petition of Hsien Tso-pang and thirteen others states, 'we are fed worse than dogs, and are called upon to perform labour for which an ox or a horse would not possess sufficient strength. Everywhere cells exist, and whips and rods are in constant use, and maimed and lacerated limbs are daily to be seen. Almost daily, also, we hear of suicides of our countrymen who have hanged themselves, jumped into wells, cut their throats or swallowed opium.' . . .

The institution known as the 'dépôt' is named in the depositions in various ways, but these different appellations, ten in number, have reference to one establishment. This originally was created for the detention of runaway slaves, and its jurisdiction was subsequently extended to the similar cases of Chinese. To the latter were added, later, all not possessing Letters of Domicile and Cedulas, whether the absence of these documents be due to refusal of them, or loss, or withdrawal by violence; and the general cessation of their issue which has taken place of recent years has rendered liability to such arrest universal. The Chinese who declines to renew his engagement with his original employer, and who, despite the chains and the whip, in so many cases resorted to, persists in his refusal, is delivered to the dépôt to labour on Government work without remuneration until through its intervention a new contract is enforced – a process constantly repeated and calculated of course to prevent any return home and any attempt to gain a livelihood independently, and resulting in exposing to the danger of being handed over to the cruelties of the plantation – the extremest – men who, hitherto employed in other services, have escaped them.

13 REFORMS AND REACTION AT THE COURT OF PEKING

For a hundred days in 1898 a stream of reforming decrees was issued by the emperor Kuang Hsu from Peking. He instituted an annual budget and abolished official sinecures. The old classical examination system was to be replaced by one which included the study of science and of foreign government. A new system of primary and middle schools was planned, as were schools for railway engineers, naval colleges and training ships. The emperor's reforms were stimulated by China's recent and humiliating defeat in the war with Japan (1894-5); they marked the high point of the movement to defeat the foreigners by learning foreign skills. But the Hundred Days Reform became a victim of palace intrigue in which eunuchs, spies and concubines all played their part. Conservative Manchu officials supported the celebrated Empress Dowager Tzu Hsi – the Emperor's aunt – in a coup d'état to forestall her own imprisonment. The emperor was seized by guards and eunuchs and conveyed to a palace on a small island in the middle of the lake in the Imperial City; his scholar-advisers were banished or beheaded. Tzu Hsi issued a decree in his name (see below) and became Regent until her death in 1908. Her nephew, by an uneasy coincidence, was to die just one day before her.

7 July—Imperial Decree
As a measure to encourage the masses to invent new and useful things, and emulate the West in literary efforts for the benefit of the Empire, we hereby promise to give extraordinary rewards to such as write practical and useful books, invent articles of use, machinery, etc., granting to such, according to the value of their labours, either substantive or brevet official rank, hereditary nobility, or decorations, in order to encourage the spirit of emulation throughout the empire. They will also be granted certain limits of time and special facilities to enjoy the benefits of their inventions or literary efforts to the exclusion of those who might copy them, while to such as establish by their sole efforts schools, foundries, big guns and small arms factories, etc., we promise to reward such, as our dynasty has been in the habit of rewarding successful

A well-posed portrait – the Empress Dowager and Ladies of Her Court

Generals who have done extraordinary service to their country. We now command the Tsungli Yamên [the Foreign Ministry] to draw up the necessary rules and regulations in connection with the above and report upon the same at once.

16 July—Imperial Decree: on Army Retrenchment and the Backwardness of Officials

One of the most important measures of reform in the present crisis of the country is the necessity of retrenchment and economy in the present system of our army organisation. The other day we ordered the various Tartar-Generals, Viceroys and Governors of provinces to make strict investigation into the matter of their armies in order to cut down and do away with the engagement of useless soldiers, and to report speedily on the result to us. We have received many of these reports in which some recommend the cutting down of the strength of the territorial troops, others recommend the cutting down of the militia, while others again recommend that the strength of the foreign-modelled and disciplined troops be cut down, and still again there are others who declare that they have cut down all they could reasonably manage and could not cut down any more. After looking carefully over these reports from our Tartar-Generals, Viceroys and Governors of provinces it appears that, although the conditions of their various provinces are different to one another, they have not succeeded in abolishing the radical faults of the several systems and it is this that really needs reform. They have not succeeded in recommending where the sums of money that may be saved should be applied to strengthen the general whole of our armies. We therefore command that this matter be again taken up and studied and reported upon once more in a strict and honest manner, the main object being that if we can manage to cut down the expense of a single useless soldier it will mean the saving of so much to the exchequer and the prevention of waste. We desire that not only in the land but also in the naval forces intelligent and strong men be enrolled, and these are to be strictly disciplined and drilled so that whenever desired they may be forces to be relied upon to do their duty.

You are also all to continue to obey a previous edict ordering the enrolling of village militia police. This force can supplement the regular troops in suppressing traitors and overawing the desperate. Then again if we could reform the Likin [Provincial Customs] Service and strictly prevent the excise employees from swallowing up the revenues, we have in all these above noted measures the nucleus of enriching the Empire and possessing brave and reliable troops to defend the country. There are no other methods that can be superior to these for the purpose. At the present moment when our empire is undergoing such difficulties and our heart is filled with anxiety, which keeps us awake day and night because of our desire to reform the country, we always tried to treat our Ministers and officers honestly and in a straightforward manner. Why is it then that we ourselves are not treated in return honestly and frankly by our Ministers and officers? We have loaded them with honours and high responsibilities; where is their gratitude to us for them, since it requires exhortations again and again from us to remind them of their duty? Yet they continue to put a veneer over their actions in trying to deceive us! This, however, is our last exhortation to them and if we in future find again the same laziness and backwardness in aiding us in our attempts at reform that have been conspicuous before, we would like to know whether these delinquents will be able to bear the weight of our righteous indignation? Let this decree be proclaimed throughout the Empire for the information of all concerned.

21 September—Imperial Decree: the result of the coup d'état; the Emperor resigns

Our Empire is now labouring under great difficulties and, therefore it is necessary to delay the question of ordinary reforms. We have worked energetically and laboriously at our duty, day and night, so that after attending closely to a myriad of matters we have often felt much lassitude in body. This brought us to the thought that her Majesty, the Empress Dowager, Tze-hsi-tuan-yu, etc., had since the reign of the late Emperor Tung Chih twice held the regency with much success, and that although the Empire was then also labouring under great difficulties she always issued triumphant and successful when grappling with critical questions. Now we consider the safety of the Empire handed down to us by our Imperial Ancestors above all things else; hence under the critical condition of things now pending over us we have thrice petitioned her Majesty to graciously accede to our prayer and personally give us the benefit of her wise instructions in the government of this Empire. She has, fortunately for the prosperity of the officials and inhabitants of the Empire, granted our request and, from today on, her Majesty will conduct the affairs of

State in the ordinary Thronehall – where the full Court etiquette is not observed, and where the sovereign may converse more freely with those having audience of him or her. We intend, therefore, at the head of our Princes and Ministers to pay our allegiance and obeisances to her Majesty on the 23rd instant, at the Ch'ang-chêng Throne-hall, and hereby command that the Board concerned shall prepare everything and also draw up a report as to what ceremonies should be observed on the said occasion.

14 THE IRON MAN OF THE BOXER REBELLION

In the northern province of Shantung there were floods and famine in 1898. The countryside was infested with bands of unemployed ex-soldiers. Shantung had just become a German 'sphere of influence', foreign consumer goods – cotton yarns, matches, paraffin – poured in and caused severe unemployment among local cottage industries. Many peasants know perfectly well, wrote a sympathetic American missionary, that 'before foreign trade came in to disturb the ancient order of things, there was in ordinary years enough to eat and wear, whereas now there is a scarcity in every direction, with a prospect of worse to come'. These were exactly the right conditions for a secret society, as so often in previous times of oppression and famine, to surface and make rebellion. The Boxers, so called because they practised a ritual form of Chinese boxing which (it was believed) could make the most expert among them become invulnerable to sword or bullet, were partly anti-Manchu but mostly anti-foreign. The Manchu court hesitated to suppress them, and in June 1900 the foreign legations in Peking were reinforced without Chinese permission. Then, with some encouragement from the Empress Dowager, they were besieged by the Boxers. The 'Siege of Peking' ended with Western intervention, more concessions to the foreign powers, and the suppression of the Boxers. Half a century later, Tung Yao, a 92-year-old peasant from near Peking, told this story, by now a folk legend, of how the Iron Man of the Boxers was betrayed by the Empress Dowager.

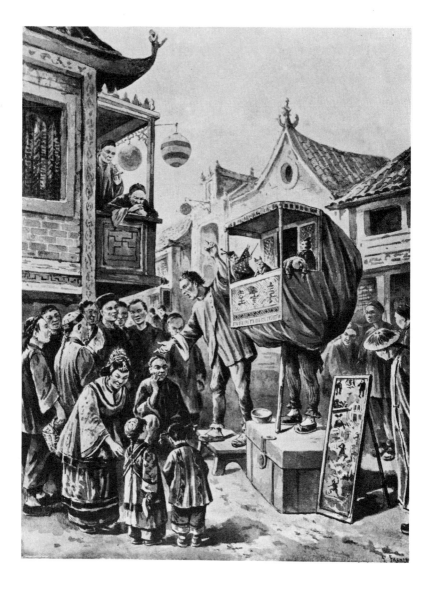

*Anti-foreign satire in a street puppet-show at the time of the Boxer Rising,
1900*

From a collection of Boxer folk-tales, Chinese Literature, *January 1960*

Once there was a fearless young fellow called Tieh Erh-leng, a tiller of the soil. He was poor enough to begin with, this Tieh Erh-leng, and poorer still after the tax-collectors came down upon him for grain and money; so when there was a great drought in the sixth month of that year matters became really desperate!

As the crops shrivelled and died, Tieh was just as worried as everyone else. But one day he had an idea. He went to Dragon King Temple at the end of the village and wagged his finger at the Dragon King:

'Listen to me, Dragon King! I've two things to say. First, I give you three days to send a good fall of rain; secondly, I want to be changed into a man whom nobody dares trample underfoot! If you agree, well and good. If not, three days from now I'll tear down your temple!'

Well, now! In those days there was a saying: Good men build temples, evil men destroy them. Anyone who tore down a temple was asking for trouble.

But do you know what? Tieh's threat had some effect: that night the Dragon King appeared to him in a dream.

'Tieh Erh-leng!' said the Dragon King. 'Whatever you do, you mustn't tear down my temple. You shall have your wish – or rather, one of them. Which would you prefer, a good fall of rain or strength so great that no sword or bullet can harm you?'

Tieh thought: If there's a good rain and we get in a crop, it will only be taken away from us by the officials. If I have enough strength no one will dare to bully me. 'All right!' he said. 'Give me strength so great that no sword or bullet can harm me.'

'That's easy. Starting tomorrow, the sky will be overcast for three whole days: there will be thunder and lightning but no rain. Just go to the river bank south of the village and stay there for three days and three nights.'

'Three days and nights are nothing,' said Tieh. 'I wouldn't mind thirty.'

The next day Tieh rose early and went to the river. At once the sky grew black as the bottom of a pan; the next instant lightning flashed and thunder crashed. The lightning struck Tieh and burned him, the thunderbolts smashed right on him! He saw stars, his heart and belly stung like fire, from head to foot he felt stabbing, shooting pains. In agony, he crawled to the river and thirstily gulped the water. So three bitter days and three bitter nights went by.

Suddenly, on the fourth morning, the sky cleared. And suddenly Tieh felt as if he were walking on air. Striding towards the village he ran full tilt into a lad. 'Hey, brother!' cried Tieh. 'Go and fetch a chopper, will you?'

'What do you want it for, elder brother?' asked the boy.

'Bring a big, sharp chopper and take a whack at me – any place you like.'

'Are you mad?' The lad backed fearfully away.

Tieh lost his temper. 'If you won't do this for me, I'll do it for you!'

The lad's hair stood on end, he took to his heels. 'Tieh Erh-leng's gone mad!' he shouted as he ran. 'He wants to kill me! Help!' The whole village turned out to see what the noise was about. They surrounded the boy and asked what the trouble was. One old man said: 'Tieh Erh-leng is straight: he's never done a crooked thing in his life. If he wants you to hack at him, he must have his reasons. Give him a couple of taps with the blunt side of the chopper and see what happens – at worst you can't do more than bruise him.'

By now Tieh had come alongside. Feeling safety in numbers, the lad took the old man's advice. He tapped Tien with the blunt side of the chopper.

'That's no use!' bellowed Tieh. 'Hit harder!' The lad put a little strength into the next blow. 'Pah! A flea-bite!' shouted Tieh. 'Can't you do better than that?' The lad hit harder and harder, but still Tieh went on complaining while the villagers stood gaping. At last the lad grew frantic, and curiosity got the better of him. Flicking over the chopper, he struck this time with the sharp side, leaving a white mark on Tieh's skin. He swung the chopper and smashed it down again. Soon he was sweating, the blade of the chopper was bent, but not a single hair of Tieh's body was hurt! The villagers cried out in wonder: 'A man of iron!' So Iron Man became Tieh's name after that.

'All I wanted was to test my strength,' he told them. 'My wish has really come true. So much the better. Next time the tax-collectors come demanding grain or money, don't give them a thing. If they ask why, tell them that's what the Iron Man said. If that doesn't satisfy them, send them to me!'

With such backing, his neighbours were afraid of nothing. And this wasn't the only village to follow his lead: once the news had spread many other villages started doing what the Iron Man said. . . .

[Tieh prevents the local magistrate from raising taxes, and chases away all the foreigners. Later they return with troops to fight the Boxers. The Iron Man, unarmed, bars their way at the head of a crowd of peasants.]

'I'd like a taste of those toys of yours, your foreign rifles and cannon,' said the Iron Man. 'But you needn't fire at such a crowd of us: first try them out on me!' He made his men withdraw, and stood there as a target for the foreign troops. 'Try your foreign rifles first!' He slapped his chest.

His fearlessness goaded them to fury. Bang, bang, bang! A volley rang out. But do you know what? The bullets simply made white marks on his skin and whizzed away, sending off sparks. After some time the foreign devils stopped, their eyes nearly starting from their heads.

The Iron Man slapped his chest again. 'Try your foreign cannon now!'

Fuming with rage, the foreign troops trained their cannon on him. Boom, boom! But do you know what? When the shells struck the Iron Man, a column of smoke shot right up into the sky, sputtering, crackling and making a braver show than the fireworks at New Year.

After a furious burst of cannon-fire, the foreign troops were sure the Iron Man must be dead. They stopped firing and had a look – there he was standing, exactly the same as before, except that his clothes were in rags and his face was blackened with smoke. His teeth gleamed white as he laughed at them!

The foreign devils began to be afraid.

The Iron Man took a step forward and grabbed a foreign rifle from one of them. Crack! – he broke the thing in two and laughed aloud. 'This isn't even up to a beggar's stick!' He tossed the broken rifle aside and picked up a foreign cannon. After taking a look, he tightened his grip and – crash! – it smashed into smithereens. He laughed long and loud again. 'This isn't as strong as a clod of Chinese earth!' He let the broken bits of the cannon fall.

The foreign devils were rooted to the ground with fear. . . .

'Charge!' The Iron Man signed to his men and was the first to charge the foreign troops, seizing foreign rifles and foreign cannon with one hand, while dealing mighty blows with his other fist. His men streamed after him, thrusting, hacking, mowing down the enemy. Not till all the foreign devils were killed or wounded or had fled did they stay their hands. Then, the Iron Man at their head, they occupied Langfang and hoisted the great banner of the Boxers.

The next day the magistrate came in his sedan-chair with an escort to see the Iron Man.

With a smile, the magistrate said: 'General Tieh, the empress dowager has sent you an edict.'

Now the capital had already been occupied by the foreigners who had put the empress dowager to flight. The imperial edict announced that the court intended to sue for peace, and therefore the Boxers must kill no more foreigners. The Iron Man was ordered to lay down arms.

'Hand that edict over to me!' In a rage the Iron Man snatched it and tore it to shreds. Pointing at the magistrate, he shouted: 'Here we've already killed all these foreign devils, yet you want to sue for peace! You are a disgrace to China! Get out of here!' He aimed a kick at the magistrate which sent him flying eighty feet through the air like a ball of donkey-dung. Officials had such a healthy respect for the Iron Man by now that, leaving his sedan-chair, the magistrate fled with his followers, not daring to look behind.

Once back in the *yamen* [magistrate's court], the magistrate wrote a memorial to the throne, and sent a horseman off with it that same night.

This memorial set the empress dowager worrying, and she consulted her most trusted ministers. One of them said: 'This Iron Man must be an evil spirit sent to trouble the world. Isn't there a worthy Buddhist abbot appointed by Your Majesty to the Temple of the Guardian of the State? He has experience in casting out evil spirits. Why not send for him?'

At once the empress dowager sent for this abbot.

The abbot said: 'A man like that will not submit to the laws till you destroy his strength. I have a charm here which, if burned to ashes and given him to eat, will enable us to chop off the fellow's head!'

'Let me go and see the Iron Man,' proposed the minister. 'I know how to handle him.' He outlined his plan to the empress dowager, who appointed him a high commissioner. Then he rode off with an escort towards Langfang.

Half-way there he met the Iron Man and his brothers.

The minister made haste to greet him. 'Where are you going, General Tieh?'

The Iron Man responded angrily: 'You spineless officials have let the foreign devils take our capital. Now that we've killed all the foreign devils behind us, we're on our way to Peking. We're going to kill the foreigners and drive them all away from the capital. They shan't have it their own way in China!'

The minister said with an ingratiating smile: 'General Tieh, you are a hero, a true defender of the state! What a lucky meeting! The empress dowager sent me out with these troops to find you. She wants your Boxers to join forces with us and march quickly to the capital to kill all the foreigners. Then she can return to her capital and the country will be at peace.'

When the Iron Man heard this he answered gladly: 'That sounds more like an empress dowager! You can count on me!'

Since dusk was falling, the minister and the Iron Man put up with the Boxers and soldiers at a large inn.

At once the minister ordered a feast and invited the Iron Man to drink with him. Men with no guile in their hearts do not suspect others – how could the Iron Man guess that the minister would slip the ashes of that charm into one of his dishes?

No sooner had the Iron Man eaten that dish than his heart began to burn, his head to reel, his eyes to grow dim and his limbs to falter. At once the minister showed his true colours. Coldly he laughed, and shouted: 'Here, men! Cut off the Iron Man's head and take it to the empress dowager!'

So by this dastardly plot the Iron Man met his end.

That night when the Boxers were sleeping, the minister assembled his soldiers by stealth and ordered: 'Put all these Boxers to the sword! Then we can make peace with the foreigners and the empress dowager can return to her capital.'

The proverb says: 'Easy to parry a spear-thrust in the open, but hard to evade an arrow shot in the dark.' That is how this force of Boxers was defeated.

15 THE MAN WHO BUILT THE FIRST CHINESE RAILWAY

The total length of China's railways was 195 miles in 1895, 2700 miles in 1903, and nearly 5800 miles in 1911 when the Manchu Empire

玉近年物兒威將侯前一切威
見雖不能破除盡淨然運會
至而風氣開擀蓬墓時之劫挢
達吳同治庫年火車已摩行
於滬導由上海達吳淞三十餘
里歷近不踰二刻惜為當道所
阻議實造作之費遠威劫
許折育下旬天津恾恔之創
辦鐵路一節　朝廷業已兄洼
由大沽至天津先行鐵辦胡
於八月二十三日患　朝史久碩
敕爽辦天津通州鐵路甚火
車式樣前一乘為機器車由具
而下威乘人或萊貨挒一二千乘
均可拖帶將來更漸推廣各
省通行一如電綫一四通八達
上與下刻蝻巽窺竊不禁我
目侸之矣

*The foreigners and their railway. A Chinese impression from
a Shanghai magazine, 1884*

興辦鉄路

was finally overthrown. But railway construction was not just a matter of improving communications; from the start it became entangled in an intricate web of international politics and high finance. After China's defeat by Japan in the war of 1894-5 the foreign powers began what was known as the 'scramble for con-concessions'. Russia, France, Germany, Britain and Japan all successfully demanded the right to finance and to build railways in the areas of China which they claimed as their 'spheres of influence'. Other lines were financed by American and Belgian interests. The Imperial government in Peking was powerless to prevent the scramble. Partly in order to keep foreign interests at bay, attempts began to be made in various Chinese provinces to construct their own railways. In 1911 the Imperial government took over a number of uncompleted local projects, raising a loan to finish their construction from an international consortium of bankers. The storm of protest which this aroused, especially in Szechwan province, led directly to the Revolution of October 1911 and the collapse of the Manchu dynasty. Here is the story of two lines which were successfully built by the Chinese, but only because the foreign powers could not agree on who was entitled to the 'concession'.

From an article in China Reconstructs, *July 1955*

Tens of thousands of visitors, Chinese and foreign, go up by rail from Peking each year to see the Great Wall of China. All are impressed, during the four-hour trip, by the steep grades the train climbs in the mountains, and by the many tunnels through which it passes.

At Chinglungchiao (Blue Dragon Bridge), the station at the foot of the Wall, the first thing they see is an imposing bronze statue of a stocky, middle-aged man in western clothes of the beginning of the present century. It is a memorial to Chan Tien-yu (known abroad as Tien Yow Jeme), China's earliest railway engineer. Fifty years ago, he planned and led the construction of this difficult line, not only up to the Great Wall but also beyond it to Kalgan [Inner Mongolia]. It was the first important railway in China to be built without foreign capital or technical help.

Chan Tien-yu was born in 1861, in a peasant family in Kwangtung province. China, then ruled by the Manchu emperors, was smarting under defeats by western invaders in the Opium Wars of 1840 and 1858-60. These disasters had cost her dearly in territory and loss of sovereignty. A 'foreignising' faction at court thought the adoption of modern techniques would strengthen the dynasty militarily. They approved the plan of the reformist Yung Hung (Yung Wing) to 'select and send children to study in the United States'.

The feudal aristocrats and landlords of those days did not want to send their sons abroad, so children of families in modest circumstances were enrolled. Chan Tien-yu was one of those who passed the preparatory examination. In 1873, when he was twelve years old, he and thirty other young boys set sail for America. Until 1878, Chan Tien-yu attended New Haven High School, in the state of Connecticut. He passed on to the Sheffield Scientific School of Yale University, where he took up civil engineering with special emphasis on railway building. He was graduated at the age of twenty in 1881, emerging at the head of his class in mathematics.

During his studies Chan Tien-yu concluded that mechanised mass production was what made the capitalist countries powerful. To learn all they had to teach about railways, he believed, was his patriotic duty, since it would help to overcome the weakness of China and the discrimination to which Chinese living abroad were subjected. Besides technical matters, he became interested in western literature – his favourite authors being Shakespeare, Boccaccio and Mark Twain.

In China, in the meantime, the conservatives launched an attack on the 'foreignising' faction and its plans. They claimed that the boys who had been sent abroad would be corrupted morally, become insubordinate, and lose their respect for ancient tradition. In 1881 the students were ordered home. Only Chan Tien-yu and one other lad came back with a college degree.

Soon afterwards, the benighted Manchu autocracy pulled up the Shanghai-Woosung railway, the only one China then had, because it 'disturbed the immortal spirits'. So for seven years, Chan Tien-yu did not practise his profession at all. Instead he was sent to learn navigation at the Imperial Naval Academy at Foochow, and later assigned to a warship. . . .

It was again characteristic of the decaying Manchu regime that when it finally undertook to build a railway on its own initiative, it was neither for public welfare nor for national defence. In 1902 the Empress Dowager, then the actual ruler of the country, ordered a short stretch built from Peking to Hsiling. This was so the imperial family could pay homage to its ancestors who were buried there. The foreign powers, however, did not want to see even this 29-mile line built without their participation. The British and French embassies each applied pressure for the appointment of a chief construction engineer of its own nationality. Since they could not settle their dispute, they had to agree to a Chinese handling the job. Chan Tien-yu got the post.

Only four winter months remained before the day of imperial ancestor-worship. Surveying, building, test-runs of trains – all had to be done during this brief period. Chan Tien-yu borrowed old bent rails, which had to be straightened, from the Peking-Mukden line. He was supplied with so few sleepers that they had to be spaced further apart than usual. Working fifteen hours a day, he and his men completed the work on time.

It was in the construction of the Peking-Kalgan line, in 1905-9, that Chan Tien-yu proved his outstanding ability as an engineer and administrator. Kalgan (Changchiakou) was one of the entry points to Inner Mongolia. Through it, a large traffic was carried on by caravans of camels and horses. Chinese merchants engaged in the trade wanted to build a railway between this town and Peking. But since they could not scrape up the capital, they requested the government to do it, using its profits from the Peking-Mukden line, a Sino-British enterprise, to finance the construction.

Once again there were diplomatic complications. London insisted that a British engineer be put in charge – because the money it was proposed to use was on deposit in the British Hongkong and Shanghai Banking Corporation. Czarist Russia objected on the grounds of an understanding she had with the Manchu regime. Under its terms, no railway running north of the Great Wall – and therefore close to Russia's borders – could be built or financed except by either herself or China. After a year's negotiations involving all three countries, it was decided that the Peking-Kalgan railway should be a Chinese enterprise.

Because of the hard country the line was to run over, a British expert declared in London that 'the engineer who can build it has not yet been born in China'. But Chan Tien-yu, who was appointed chief engineer and vice-director, had no doubts. 'It's true that we haven't many engineers,' he said, 'but that doesn't matter. As long as we have workers and administrators, I can help them and they can help me. Together we can do the job.'

The obstacles were indeed formidable. On the south section, between Peking and the famous Nankow Pass in the Great Wall, high mountains and sheer precipices barred the way. At some points the survey parties could not even find a foothold, much less place for a roadbed.

Defeatists and worshippers of everything foreign, of whom there were many in the Manchu government, ridiculed Chan Tien-yu as 'foolish and rash', as a man who 'did not know his own limitations'. But he paid no attention. Going out with the survey parties himself, he climbed the jagged mountains amid dust-storms and howling winds, and finally marked out the route. At night, when all were asleep, he sat awake making drawings and calculations. He was determined to do an above-standard job at less than the rated cost, to show that China could not only build but do it economically.

While the dapper government supervisors sat around all day, smoking and drinking tea, Chan Tien-yu climbed into overalls and mixed with the workers. He both helped them and learned from their suggestions, never putting on airs. Old peasants in the area still remember 'Commissioner Chan', so unlike the usual imperial official, riding up and down on a mule with surveying instruments strapped to his back. The line, as finally laid out, was shorter than the best distance estimated by foreign engineers.

16 SUN YAT-SEN ACHIEVES HIS LIFE'S AMBITION

In October 1911 Sun Yat-sen was on a tour of the United States, raising money from overseas Chinese and foreign sympathisers for the revolutionary cause. His organisation (the forerunner of the Kuomintang or Chinese Nationalist Party which was first set up in August 1912) was mostly supported by Chinese students and exiles abroad, and the rebellions which it had previously inspired in China had not been marked by success. It was somehow characteristic that Sun, already known internationally as the leader of the Chinese revolution, should have been out of touch when the real revolution took place. It was also characteristic that Sun, as he narrates in this extract, should have felt obliged to stop off in London on his way home and negotiate with the foreign bankers. The Republican ideology was provided by Sun, but the military over-

Soon in opposition again after the 1911 Revolution, Sun died before the Kuomintang could regain power. Here Sun is seen in 1923 with his successor, Chiang Kai-shek

throw of the Manchu dynasty was made possible by the defection of the New Armies which, ironically, had been established through the dynasty's own reluctant reforms. When the Revolution broke out, the Imperial Court instructed General Yuan Shih-k'ai to 'suppress the bandits'. Instead he negotiated with the rebels, and forced the Manchu emperor to abdicate. Sun recognised the military realities of the situation. A month after he had been elected President of the Republic in Nanking, he resigned in favour of Yuan Shih-k'ai in Peking. The new democratic order was placed in the hands of the first, but not the last, Chinese warlord.

From Sun Yat-sen's Memoirs of a Chinese Revolutionary

While the rising was taking place at Wuchang [October 1911], I arrived in Columbia. Ten days before my arrival there, I received a telegram from Huang Hsing from Hongkong, but as the cipher was in my baggage, I could not read the telegram, and only deciphered it when I arrived in one of the towns of the State of Columbia. The telegram stated that Tsui Chen had arrived at Kongkong and reported that money was necessary to assist the rising of the recently mobiled soldiers. Being in Columbia, I had not any money, of course, and could not procure it, and intended to send a telegram postponing the rising. But night fell, and, being tired by my journey, I postponed it till the morning, in order to think over the question again with a clear head. I woke up the next morning at 11 o'clock and, being hungry, went out to a restaurant. On my way I bought a newspaper and, arriving at the restaurant, unfolded it; immediately my eyes were met by a telegram about the capture of Wuchang by the revolutionary troops. I thereupon sent a detailed telegram to Huang Hsing, in which I explained the reason for my silence.

In twenty days I could come to Shanghai and take a personal part in the revolutionary struggle, but for us our diplomatic front was more important even than the military front for the moment. Therefore, I decided to concentrate my efforts on diplomatic affairs, only after settling this business to return home. . . .

Thus, the international sympathy was a question of importance for the Chinese Revolution. The most important of all for us, at the moment, was the attitude of England; for we considered that if England took our side Japan would not delay in following her example. Therefore, I decided to leave for England.

When going through St Louis, I read a newspaper statement to the effect that a revolution had broken out at Wuchang and that in the proposed Republic Sun Yat-sen would be the President. After this I had to hide from the Press correspondents, as it turned out that rumour was in advance of fact.

Accompanied by comrade Chu Tso-wen, I continued my long journey to England. On arrival in New York, I received information that the comrades were making an attack on Canton, and I sent a telegram to Governor Chang Ming-ch'i proposing that he should surrender the city, in order to avoid bloodshed, and ordered the comrades to grant him his life, which was later on carried out.

On my arrival in England, I entered through my English friend into negotiations with the Banking Consortium of the Four Powers, with a view to stopping all loans for the Imperial Manchu House. The position was that the Consortium had already granted one loan of a hundred millions on the security of the Chuan-Han [Szechwan-Hankow] Railway, and then a further loan of a hundred millions.[1] On one of these loans the money had already been partly paid, but on the other, although the signature was appended, the bonds had not yet been issued. My intention was to secure the stoppage of payment on the loan which had been carried through, and to prevent the issue of bonds for the other loan. I knew that the settlement of this depended on the Foreign Secretary, and therefore I instructed the Director of the Wei-Hai-Wei Arsenal to enter into negotiations with the British Government on three questions, on the settlement of which I insisted. The first was the annulment of all loans to the Tai-Tsing [Manchu] dynasty. The second was to prevent Japan from helping the dynasty, and the third was to withdraw all orders prohibiting me from entering British territory [i.e. Hongkong], so that I could return to China more conveniently.

Having received a favourable settlement of these questions from the British Government, I then turned to the Banking Consortium to secure a loan for the revolutionary Government. I received the following reply from the manager of the Consortium: 'Since the Government has stopped the loans for the dynasty, our Consortium will grant these loans only to a firmly-established and officially-recognised Government. The Consortium proposes for the present to send a representative with you on your return, and when the official recognition of your Government takes place, it will be possible

[1]The correct figures are actually £6 million for the 'Hukuang Railways Loan', and £10 million for the 'Currency Loan'.

to open negotiations.' This was all I could do during my stay in England. I then returned home through France, and during my passage through Paris met representatives of the French Opposition Parties. I received expressions of sympathy from all, particularly from Premier Clemenceau. Thirty days after my departure from France I arrived at Shanghai. The Peace Conference of South and North was taking place at this time, but the Constitution of the future Republic was not yet determined.

Even before my arrival at Shanghai, all the foreign and Chinese newspapers were spreading widely the story that I was returning home with a large sum of money to help the Revolution. When I arrived at Shanghai, both my comrades and the reporters of the foreign and Chinese newspapers expected this, but I replied that I had not brought with me a farthing: but had brought with me a revolutionary spirit, and that, until the aim of the Revolution had been achieved, there could be no question of peace conferences.

Soon after this the deputies from all the provinces of China, assembled in the city of Nanking, elected me Provisional President of China. In 1912 I assumed office, and ordered the Proclamation of the Chinese Republic, the alteration of the lunar calendar, and the declaration of that year as the First Year of the Chinese Republic.

Thus thirty years passed as one day, and only after their completion did I achieve my principal aim, the aim of my life – the creation of the Chinese Republic.

17 A WARLORD ASCENDS THE THRONE

China's newborn democratic republic, born in 1912, was soon throttled by President Yuan Shih-k'ai. By the end of 1913 Sun Yat-sen's Kuomintang Party had been dissolved and one of its leaders assassinated. Yuan's election as President was confirmed after the Peking secret police had surrounded Parliament and threatened its members. Parliament itself was then dissolved. Yuan brought in a new constitution giving him full powers and a ten-year term of office, with the opportunity to be re-elected at the end of it. Meanwhile he accepted several crippling foreign loans in order to buy support both from the Western powers and from rival militarists in China. Finally Yuan set his sights on the highest honour, this time over-reaching himself. In the following extract a distinguished Chinese historian writing in the West, Dr Jerome Ch'en, describes how the President became – for exactly eighty-three days – Emperor. Another revolution was launched, Yuan's supporters turned against him, and the 'strong man of China' died within weeks of disappointment. And the already fragile institutions of Chinese democracy were wrecked beyond repair.

From Jerome Ch'en's Yuan Shih-k'ai

A significant anecdote was circulating among Yuan's officers in 1915:

Yuan had a habit of taking a short nap after lunch and having a cup of tea immediately afterwards. A boy was given the job of bringing the tea.

One day when the boy went into the bedroom, carrying the tea in an exquisite jade cup, he saw, not his master, but a huge toad sitting on the couch. Stunned, he dropped the cup on the floor. Fortunately, the noise did not disturb the sleeping president.

The boy tiptoed out of the room and then ran to an elderly servant who treated him as a son. He told the old man what had happened and tearfully begged him to make up some story that would keep Yuan from punishing him for breaking the valuable cup. The old man pondered a while and then told the child what to say, should their master ask any questions.

Presently, Yuan woke up to find his tea in a porcelain beaker. He at once summoned the boy and asked him where the jade cup was. The boy answered truthfully.

'Broken?' Yuan's tone was severe. But the boy calmly explained, 'Yes, Sir, because I saw something very strange.' 'What?' demanded the master, visibly annoyed. 'When I came in here a moment ago with a cup of tea, I did not see you, Sir, on the couch, but . . .' 'But what? You liar!' 'But a five-clawed golden dragon.' 'Rubbish!' the master shouted, but his anger suddenly left him. He opened a drawer, took out a hundred-dollar bill, and thrust it into the boy's hand. He cautioned him not to mention a word of what he had just seen to anyone else.

The story reflected a widely held belief that Yuan was about to try to found a dynasty; it also ridiculed his faith in superstition. The popularity that this unflattering anecdote enjoyed in military circles was ominous for Yuan. . . .

Toward the end of November, preparations neared completion.

PRESIDENT YUAN SHIH-KAI,
FIRST PRESIDENT OF THE REPUBLIC OF CHINA.

Yuan Shih-k'ai, first President of Republican China, in full regalia

Another confidential telegram was sent out to the generals and governors:

The following words must be included in your messages exhorting the president to accept the throne: 'We, the representatives of the people, represent the true wishes of the whole nation in urging the present president, Yuan Shih-k'ai, to assume the title of emperor and in giving him all the powers of an emperor. May Heaven save him. May his sons and grandsons inherit this position for a myriad of generations to come.'

The last of the monarchists' communications read:

No matter how careful we are, some of the communications between us may survive as permanent records. Once they are known to outsiders, we cannot hope to escape severe criticism and attacks, which will mar the opening chapter of the history of the new dynasty. After careful deliberation, the central government has decided that all the communications should be burned. . . . Please supervise the destruction in person.

The messages were destroyed on 29 March 1916. But long before that the National Congress of Representatives had been convoked. The 1993 members unanimously voted for the adoption of a monarchial system and for Yuan's elevation to the throne. All the votes bore the precise wording specified in the November telegram. Chou Tzu-ch'i, a confidant of Yuan's, later told [US ambassador] Reinsch, 'We tried to get some people to vote against the monarchy just for appearance's sake, but they would not do it.' Chou was obviously trying to impress his American listener with the people's enthusiasm for the proposed change.

The vote took place on 21 November. On 12 December, the Council of State, acting on a resolution proposed by Prince P'u-lun, presented a 3000-word *memorial* urging the president to accept the throne. In so doing, the council was acting as a legislative body, which in fact it was not. The memorial was written in the style of the *Book of Rites* and addressed the president as 'Your Holy Majesty'. The president gave his customary show of modesty by refusing it. Fifteen minutes later, another memorial of equal length was ready for presentation; it began by insisting that he accept the Mandate of Heaven. Yuan graciously accepted that very day.

Hsü Shih-ch'ang, the minister of state and Yuan's sworn-brother, at once fell ill; his duties were taken over by Lu Cheng-hsiang. On 15 December, the president made General Li Yuan-hung a prince in a decree bearing the presidential seal. This seal, however, disappeared from Yuan's decrees two days later. General Feng

Kuo-chang, whose lukewarm attitude toward the monarchy had not pleased Yuan, was ordered to leave his governorship in Nanking to fill Li's old post of chief-of-staff. Both Li and Feng declined their new positions. Li was acting out of courtesy and eventually accepted. Feng, however, was trying to avoid getting entangled in Yuan's plan and losing the rich province of Kiangsu.

Following an ancient imperial example, Yuan designated Hsü Shih-ch'ang, Chao Erh-hsün, Li Ching-hsi, and Chang Chien – all of whom had resigned their posts in the government – the Four Friends of Mount Sung, the central sacred mountain in Yuan's native province of Honan. He made all his important generals dukes, marquises, or earls, fulfilling his promise to give Han Chinese noble titles.

Yuan promised the Manchu court that he would maintain the agreement made with them at the time of the abdication. (Most of the terms had been kept since then, except that the allowance had not been paid regularly.) Relations between the two courts were as amiable as could be expected. Yuan even succeeded in inducing Prince P'u-lun, the pretender to the throne whom he had supported in 1908, to kowtow to him and to call himself 'Your subject'.

An office to supervise the ceremonial details for the establishment of the new empire was set up as early as September 1915. The new dynasty was to be named Hung-hsien, which, Yuan said, meant Grand Constitutional Era. The eunuch system, according to a decree of 22 December 1915, was not to be revived; instead the new emperor would have women as his palace attendants. Early in 1916, Yuan sent one Kuo Pao-ch'ang to Kingtehchen to supervise the manufacture of 40,000 porcelain pieces for his palace, at a cost of 1.4 million *yuan*. Compared with other items, this was a small sum. The Society of Planning for Peace and Security cost Yuan from two to three million *yuan*; the redecoration of the three main palace halls, 2.7 million; two imperial robes, 800,000; and a jade seal, 120,000. The budget for the enthronement ceremony was set at six million *yuan*. It was estimated that the whole affair would cost the treasury nearly thirty million *yuan*. Where was the money to come from?

The budget for 1916 projected a deficit of nearly eighty-nine million *yuan*. Further, when the finance minister introduced the budget, he admitted that the actual revenues for the year could not be expected to exceed 150 million *yuan*, and the actual expenditures would be no less than 470 million. Under the circumstances, Yuan had to rely on borrowing and issuing irredeemable banknotes to finance the founding of his empire. Liang Shih-i, now restored to favour, was given the task of floating a loan of twenty million *yuan*, but he managed to sell bonds for only one-third of that sum. Both the Bank of China and the Bank of Communications gave Yuan generous support. Yuan also sent a trusted official to Kwangtung, ostensibly to enforce the prohibition on opium but in fact to sell the right to trade the drug.

In a cave in Ichang, Hupei, archaeologists and local officials discovered the fossil of a dinosaur, which they identified as a 'divine dragon'. The government, no doubt regarding the news as an auspicious confirmation of the mandate of Heaven, issued a formal announcement of the discovery on 15 January 1916. The foreign papers put no more faith in this omen than they did in the myth of a popular demand for change. As Sir John Jordan [British ambassador] candidly told Liang Shih-i: 'Foreigners knew perfectly well that the whole agitation was engineered from Peking'.

18 A YOUTHFUL CALL FOR LIBERATION

In 1919 a young Chinese called Mao Tse-tung wrote an article for a provincial magazine, giving it the title of 'The Great Union of the Popular Masses'. Mao had just spent six months working as a librarian in Peking University at a time of unprecedented intellectual and political ferment among his generation. Against the backcloth of China's warlord-ridden politics, young Chinese looked abroad – to the Russian revolution for Marxism, to Europe and America for democratic and socialist ideals – searching to find an answer to their country's weaknesses. They were humiliated above all by the decision of the allied powers, victorious against Germany, to let Japan take over the ex-German 'sphere of influence' in Shantung province. On 4 May 1919 Peking students demonstrated against this decision, and the movement of political and social protest which erupted became known as the May Fourth Movement. Feudal customs and the old society at home were as much a target as the foreign powers. In this article Mao Tse-tung (influenced at this time

Two demonstrations by patriotic students, Peking, May 1919. Below, police break up the meeting

more by anarchist than by Marxist ideology) argues that the various oppressed groups in Chinese society should defend their interests by getting organised into 'unions'. Peasants, workers, students, women, teachers, policemen and rickshaw boys all have the right and the power to demand 'liberation'. Fifty years later in the Cultural Revolution, the Red Guards would quote from this article by Mao to justify their own right to 'make rebellion'. And for over half a century Mao's own confidence, expressed in the conclusion to this extract, in the 'great inherent capacities' of the Chinese people has never wavered.

From The Great Union of the Popular Masses, *July 1919*

Gentlemen! We are peasants, and so we want to establish a union with others who cultivate the land as we do, in order to promote the various interests of us tillers of the soil. It is only we ourselves who can pursue the interests of us tillers of the soil; others who do not cultivate the soil have interests different from ours, and can certainly not help us to seek our interests. All you gentlemen who cultivate the land! How do the landlords treat us? Are the rents and taxes heavy or light? Are our houses satisfactory or not? Are our bellies full or not? Is there enough land? Are there not some in the village who have no land to cultivate? We must constantly seek solutions to all these problems. We must establish a union with others like ourselves, to seek clear and effective solutions.

Gentlemen! We are workers. We wish to form a union with others who work like ourselves, in order to promote the various interests of us workers. We cannot fail to seek a solution to such problems concerning us workers as the level of our wages, the length of the working day, the equal or unequal sharing of dividends, or the progress of amusement facilities. We cannot but establish a union with those like ourselves to seek clear and effective solutions to each of these problems.

Gentlemen! We are students. Our lives are extremely bitter; the professors who teach us treat us like criminals, humiliate us like slaves, lock us up like prisoners. The windows in our classrooms are so tiny that the light does not reach the blackboard, so that we become 'near-sighted'. The desks are extremely ill-adapted, and if we sit in them for very long we get 'curvature of the spine'. The professors are interested only in making us read a lot of books, and we do read a great many of them, but we don't understand any of it, we merely exercise our memories to no good purpose. Our eyes are blurred, our brains are confused, our blood supply is insufficient, our faces are ashen and we become 'anaemic'. We become 'feeble-minded'. Why are we so lethargic, so lacking in vivacity, so withered? Oh! It is all because the professors force us to refrain from moving or speaking out. And so we become 'petrified unto death'. And yet this bodily suffering is only secondary, gentlemen! Look at our laboratories! How cramped they are! How lacking in equipment! Only a few poor instruments, so that we cannot conduct experiments. Our teachers of Chinese are such obstinate pedants. They are constantly mouthing expressions such as 'We read in the *Book of Odes (Shih yun)*,' or 'The Master [Confucius] says *(Tzu yueh)*,' but when you come right down to it, the fact is, they don't understand a word. They are not aware that this is already the twentieth century, and they still compel us to observe the 'old rites', and to follow the 'old regulations'. They forcibly impregnate our minds with a lot of stinking corpse-like dead writings full of classical allusions. Our reading room is empty. Our recreation room is filthy. The country is about to perish, and yet they still stick up proclamations forbidding us to love our country. Just see, for example, what great favour they have shown to the present movement of national salvation [*i.e.,* the May Fourth Movement]! Alas! Who is it that has frustrated us and made us unhappy in both body and mind? If we do not unite in order to attend to our own 'self-instruction', then what are we waiting for? We are already sunk in an ocean of suffering, and we demand that attention be given to the means for saving ourselves. The 'self-instruction' invented by Rousseau is most appropriate for this purpose. We will unite with as many comrades as possible, and study by ourselves. As for those professors who bite people, we must not rely on them. If an event occurs such as the present trampling on our rights by the powerful people of Japan and of our own country, then we will marshal our forces and direct at them a great and powerful shout.

Gentlemen! We are women. We are even more deeply immersed in an ocean of suffering! We are also human beings, so why won't they let us take part in politics? We are also human beings, so why won't they let us participate in social intercourse? We are gathered together in our various separate dens, and we are not even allowed to go outside the front gate. The shameless men, the villainous men, make us into their playthings, and force us to prostitute ourselves to them indefinitely. The devils, who destroy the freedom to love!

The devils, who destroy the sacredness of love! They keep us surrounded all day long, but so-called 'chastity' is confined to us women! The 'temples to virtuous women' are scattered all over the place, but where are the 'pagodas to chaste men'? Among us there are some who are gathered together in schools for women, but those who teach us there are also a bunch of shameless and villainous men. All day long they talk about something called being 'a worthy mother and a good wife'. What is this but teaching us to prostitute ourselves indefinitely to the same man? They are afraid that we will not allow ourselves to be fettered, so they intensify their indoctrination. O bitterness! Bitterness! Spirit of freedom! Where are you? Come quickly and save us! Today we are awakened! We want to establish a union of us women! We want to sweep away all those devils who rape us and destroy the liberty of our minds and of our bodies!

Gentlemen! We are primary-school teachers. All day long we teach, we are terribly busy! All day long we eat chalk dust, and yet we have no place to relax. In a big city like this, there are several hundred, if not several thousand, primary-school teachers, and yet there is no place of recreation specifically set aside for our use. If we are to teach, we must constantly increase our knowledge, and yet there is no study organisation set up for our use. There are so many periods when we must go to teach precisely as the bell rings, we have absolutely no time left over, no energy left over, to study and acquire knowledge – our spirits are simply not up to it! Thus we turn into phonographs, doing nothing all day long but putting on a performance of the lectures correctly transmitted which the teachers of former days taught to us. Our bellies are hungry. Our monthly salaries are eight or ten *yuan*, and even on this there are deductions. There are some of these gentlemen among the principals who moreover imitate the method of 'reducing the soldiers' pay', and take the money provided by the government to line their own pockets. Because we have no money, we find ourselves moreover in the position of widowers with wives. We and our beloved wives live in solitude, separated by several tens or hundreds of *li*, gazing towards one another. Teaching students in a primary school is the task of a lifetime; they can hardly expect us in addition to spend all our lives as widowers and widows, can they? According to educational theory, the teachers' families should live at the school, if they are to serve as a model for the students, but today this is not possible. Because we have no money, we can't buy books either, nor can we travel and observe the world. There is no use saying any more. Primary-school teachers are in all respects slaves, and that's all there is to it! If we want to cease to be slaves, there is no way save to unite with others like ourselves, and to realise a primary-school teachers' union.

Gentlemen! We are policemen. We also wish to unite with others like ourselves, in order to realise a union which will benefit our bodies and our minds. The Japanese say that those whose lives are hardest are beggars, primary-school teachers and policemen. We are also inclined to feel somewhat the same.

Gentlemen! We are rickshaw boys. All day we pull our rickshaws until the sweat pours down like rain! The rent which goes to the owners of the rickshaws is so much! The fares we get are so small! How can we make a living? Is there not some way for us to form a union too?

The foregoing are the lamentations of the peasants, workers, students, women, primary-school teachers, rickshaw boys and others of all sorts. They are unable to bear such hardship, and so they want to set up all sorts of small unions adapted to their interests. . . .

In reality, for thousands of years the Chinese people of several hundred millions all led a life of slaves. Only one person, the 'emperor', was not a slave (or rather one could say that even he was a slave of 'heaven'). When the emperor was in control of everything, we were not allowed to exercise our capacities. Whether in politics, study, society, etc., we were not allowed to have either thought, organisation or practice.

Today things are different, and in every domain we demand liberation. Ideological liberation, political liberation, economic liberation, liberation [in the relations between] men and women, educational liberation, are all going to burst from the deep inferno where they have been confined, and demand to look at the blue sky. Our Chinese people possesses great inherent capacities! The more profound the oppression, the greater its resistance; that which has accumulated for a long time will surely burst forth quickly. I venture to make a singular assertion: one day, the reform of the Chinese people will be more profound than that of any other people, and the society of the Chinese people will be more radiant than that of any other people. The great union of the Chinese people will be achieved earlier than that of any other place or people. Gentlemen! Gentlemen! We must all exert ourselves! We must all advance with the utmost strength! Our golden age, our age of glory and splendour, lies before us!

The writer Lu Hsun at a students' meeting in Peking, 1932

19 LU HSUN AND THE NEW LITERATURE

The May Fourth Movement which sparked off a new wave of social and anti-imperialist struggle after the First World War also brought about a revolution in Chinese literature. Consciously rejecting the classical style of composition which the traditional scholars had a vested interest in preserving, young writers began to use 'plain language' (*pai-hua*), the colloquial style which could be understood without a classical education, to speak directly to a wider audience. Short stories were a popular form of political and literary self-expression in the dozens of journals which flourished in the new literature movement. Lu Hsun (Lu Xun), already a distinguished classical scholar, adopted the new style and turned later to Marxism, becoming after his death a model example for the communists of how a writer should combine his art with politics. Lu Hsun's short stories are in a class of their own, touching the raw nerves of all that was backward and evil in Chinese society in a vivid but economical style. In this story, 'An Incident', written in 1920, Lu Hsun uses the tale of a minor rickshaw accident to criticise subtly the reluctance of most Chinese intellectuals (including himself at that time) to get involved in politics and the life of the ordinary people.

Lu Hsun, 'An Incident'

Six years have slipped by since I came from the country to the capital. During that time I have seen and heard quite enough of so-called affairs of state; but none of them made much impression on me. If asked to define their influence, I can only say they aggravated my ill temper and made me, frankly speaking, more and more misanthropic.

One incident, however, struck me as significant, and aroused me from my ill temper, so that even now I cannot forget it.

It happened during the winter of 1917. A bitter north wind was blowing, but, to make a living, I had to be up and out early. I met scarcely a soul on the road, and had great difficulty in hiring a rickshaw to take me to S—Gate. Presently the wind dropped a little. By now the loose dust had all been blown away, leaving the roadway clean, and the rickshaw man quickened his pace. We were just approaching S—Gate when someone crossing the road was entangled in our rickshaw and slowly fell.

It was a woman, with streaks of white in her hair, wearing ragged clothes. She had left the pavement without warning to cut across in front of us, and although the rickshaw man had made way, her tattered jacket, unbuttoned and fluttering in the wind, had caught on the shaft. Luckily the rickshaw man pulled up quickly, otherwise she would certainly have had a bad fall and been seriously injured.

She lay there on the ground, and the rickshaw man stopped. I did not think the old woman was hurt, and there had been no witnesses to what had happened, so I resented this officiousness which might land him in trouble and hold me up.

'It's all right,' I said. 'Go on.'

He paid no attention, however—perhaps he had not heard—for he set down the shafts, and gently helped the old woman to get up. Supporting her by one arm, he asked:

'Are you all right?'

'I'm hurt.'

I had seen how slowly she fell, and was sure she could not be hurt. She must be pretending, which was disgusting. The rickshaw man had asked for trouble, and now he had it. He would have to find his own way out.

But the rickshaw man did not hesitate for a minute after the old woman said she was injured. Still holding her arm, he helped her slowly forward. I was surprised. When I looked ahead, I saw a police station. Because of the high wind, there was no one outside, so the rickshaw man helped the old woman towards the gate.

Suddenly I had a strange feeling. His dusty, retreating figure seemed larger at that instant. Indeed, the further he walked the larger he loomed, until I had to look up to him. At the same time he seemed gradually to be exerting a pressure on me, which threatened to overpower the small self under my fur-lined gown.

My vitality seemed sapped as I sat there motionless, my mind a blank, until a policeman came out. Then I got down from the rickshaw.

The policeman came up to me, and said, 'Get another rickshaw. He can't pull you any more.'

Without thinking, I pulled a handful of coppers from my coat pocket and handed them to the policeman. 'Please give him these,' I said.

The wind had dropped completely, but the road was still quiet.

I walked along thinking, but I was almost afraid to turn my thoughts on myself. Setting aside what had happened earlier, what had I meant by that handful of coppers? Was it a reward? Who was I to judge the rickshaw man? I could not answer myself.

Even now, this remains fresh in my memory. It often causes me distress, and makes me try to think about myself. The military and political affairs of those years I have forgotten as completely as the classics I read in my childhood. Yet this incident keeps coming back to me, often more vivid than in actual life, teaching me shame, urging me to reform, and giving me fresh courage and hope.

20 CIGARETTES AND EXPLOITATION IN NORTH CHINA

In the 1920s and 1930s the economic plight of the Chinese peasant grew steadily worse in most parts of the country. Higher taxes were levied from him to pay for foreign loans and warlord adventures. His sons were likely to be conscripted; his land to be plundered by marauding armies. With little or no help from the government in times of flood or famine, he was often forced to mortgage or sell his fields. As time went on the ownership of land became concentrated in fewer hands; the number of poor peasants and labourers increased. Foreign manufactured goods, allowed into China at low tariff rates which had been laid down in the 'Treaties', disturbed the domestic market economy. Cotton goods from Calcutta and Japan drove out of business the owners of thousands of local hand-looms. Rural handicrafts became more and more dependent on the city merchants and bankers to market their products, and prices could fluctuate wildly. In some areas the peasants were encouraged to switch their production to cash crops like tobacco, silk or peanuts, only to find themselves at the mercy of the big manufacturing companies and their middlemen. This article describes the activities of the British American Tobacco Company in a part of North China where it persuaded whole districts to take up tobacco planting. This company produced more than half the tobacco in China but (as the *Chinese Yearbook* for 1935-6 recorded) it 'has consistently preserved great secrecy about everything that concerns itself'.

Hsu Yung-sui, article translated in Agrarian China, *1939*

In the middle of October 1936 the writer of the present article was sent with his colleagues to collect tobacco leaves in the production regions of eastern Shantung. As this was his first experience in this field, all experience was as fresh as it was instructive. Here the condition of the tobacco peasants and their subjugation by the power of industrial capital were brought home to him so forcefully that they left an indelible impression.

The first industrial company to operate in this tobacco district was a foreign one which, as early as 1915, distributed American tobacco seed in the villages along the Tsingtao-Chinan Railway. At first only about one-tenth of the peasant families in the tobacco regions used these seeds, but as the alluring price convinced them that no other agricultural product could yield the same return, more and more peasant families, as far as their means would permit, took up tobacco cultivation. The development has been so fast that at present at the eastern end of the railway, west of Fong-tze and east of Chow-ts'un, one-fifth of a million *mow* are planted with American seed. Travelling along the railway, one cannot fail to be impressed by the vast fields of large golden leaves.

Many peasants took up tobacco cultivation, not primarily because of the expected returns but rather because, in the midst of their poverty, tobacco planting was the only way to obtain seed and loans. For this reason agriculture in eastern Shantung is rapidly being commercialised and as this process goes on the prices of commercial crops affect the lives of the peasants to an ever greater extent. The peasants are not unaware of this, but forced by circumstances they have to gamble on the crop which has put them in the grip of the price manipulators.

The growth of tobacco from seedling to harvest takes about ninety days, from May to the middle of August. After harvesting the leaves are baked in an underground house kept at a definite temperature. This is a bare house of about eight feet square, without light. It is thickly hung with tobacco leaves which are usually looked after by a woman, who stays there throughout the baking process. If it were possible to look into such a house one would probably see a figure with dirty face and uncombed hair, wearing a pair of red trousers tied tightly just above her tiny feet. She has to watch the leaves for about a week, being most of the time on her feet, and all the time in the hot, moist atmosphere. When baking is finished, the leaves are taken out to be sorted according to their lustre and each leaf is inspected before tying them in bunches of five or six. All this involves a great deal of labour. More than ten days are necessary for one person to handle the leaves from one *mow*.

The total cost of production per *mow* usually amounts to eighty-five dollars including the cost of seedlings, bean cake fertiliser, coal for the leaf baking, cash wages and taxes. This far exceeds the cost of grain production, for not counting other items, cash has to be laid out to buy the coal. Thus the tobacco producers are forced to make loans, the prevailing form being in credit purchases. The usual monthly interest is three per cent, but it is often higher than this. Loans have to be guaranteed, not excepting credit purchases. While the cash price for bean cake fertiliser is $1.10 per piece, 10 cents more is charged in the case of credit purchases, which must be paid within six months.

The collection of tobacco leaves begins in October when tobacco merchants connected with factories from different directions come to the production region. Suddenly every collection station is turned into a very busy market with colourful banners flying on high poles to announce the agencies of the different business concerns. Nearby, various shops are set up for the season, carrying in their stock numerous varieties of cheap Japanese goods, chiefly porcelain and cloth. Some of these shops operate victrolas, playing discarded and obsolete records to attract the crowd. These shops, however, have no easy time with their peasant customers who, owing to their financial stringency and consequent caution, will not buy anything until they have gone through a long process of bargaining. Almost every bargain is only made as a result of persistent persuasion from the shopkeeper and frequent visits by the customer.

During the collection season, long processions of wheelbarrows and carts drawn by oxen or horses move slowly along the winding, bumpy and dusty roads. The transportation of tobacco leaves to the market is made more difficult by the wind which frequently rises, carrying with it the thick, yellow dust which makes the way hard to find. At other times, sudden storms reduce the roads to thick mud which makes it hard for wheels to move, and huge pools form through which the peasants have to wade. To cover distances of as much as thirty miles over such roads is no mean feat, and considering further the food and other accommodations that have to be found for the journey, carrying the tobacco leaves to the market becomes a large item of cost to the producers themselves. The sig-

Two woodcuts (from a collection made by Lu Hsun) tell the story of the 1930s. Above, 'Struggle' by Tai Lo; right, 'People on the Roof-tops' by Li Hua

nificance of the price received for the leaves, therefore, has to be weighed against the cost of production and transportation combined, and even the slightest difference in that price arouses in the peasant a surging wave of emotion carrying with it all the vivid reflections of his physical toil and suffering.

Arriving at the leaf collection ground, the peasants have to line up in one of the many queues, some of which are as long as two-thirds of a mile. Confusion seems unavoidable and the police beat them into line with thonged whips. Exposed to hunger and cold they have to wait with the utmost patience, and those standing at the ends of the queues often have to wait for twenty-four hours and even then are unable to push through the crowd to the doors. Every year there are tragic incidents; some get trampled down by the crowd, some are fatally injured, being rammed by the shafts of the carts, and occasionally boys who are too young to hold their own in the crowd get smothered.

The collection house resembles a big barn with rows of wooden counters covered with bamboo stretchers upon which the peasants have to dump their leaves. Being afraid that the leaves will dry up and lose their lustre in the long interval before the inspector comes round, the peasants often take off their coats, in spite of the cold, and use them to cover the leaves. They stand there with outstretched necks and tense expressions, eagerly awaiting the inspector who, in their minds, is the pronouncer of the final verdict of fortune or doom for the following twelve months. When the inspector finally arrives he quickly classifies the leaves by inspecting a few bunches, but if the peasant should hesitate to sell any one grade or any one stretcherful, all his leaves will be refused. Sometimes when the inspector finds several bunches of lower-grade leaves among those of a higher grade, he will confiscate the leaves as a warning. Should the peasant make any verbal protest, he gets roughly handled, and should he resist this actively, the police are immediately called in to arrest him on charges of theft or disturbance of the peace. The peasant is invariably blamed for starting any such affair and in addition to possible fine and imprisonment he is severely cautioned at the time of release.

The foreign company referred to at the beginning of this article, though maintaining its own police, gives no better treatment to the peasants than any other collecting agency. There is, however, a difference in leaf collection by this company and that of others. Whereas this concern strives for strict standardisation, without falsification of weights, and will not allow any argument or bargaining, the others tolerate negotiation but also resort to deceit in matters of weight and classification. For many years in the past when the other collecting agencies paid for the leaves with paper money, which later brought the peasants great losses, this foreign company adopted the policy of giving prompt cash. This won the credulity of the peasants as to the honesty of the foreign company, which even outweighed the risk of being paid a slightly lower price.

The largest part of upwards of $10,000,000 worth of tobacco leaves produced in eastern Shantung is collected by this foreign company which has virtual control over the entire market. Every year it has the initial power to decide the prices of leaves, and the other collectors are more or less bound to follow its lead. Thus during the years of economic depression, particularly when the Manchurian market was almost lost, it has been able to drop the collection prices of leaves on the strength of its monopoly. But what has been conceded to the consumer in the market price has been taken from the peasant producer, who has almost the entire burden shifted to him.

Due to the relatively large amount of foreign capital invested, the tobacco market in eastern Shantung is already developed to such an extent that it has a controlling influence over the entire agrarian economy of that section of the country. It is true that this particular commercial crop has already increased productivity, has enlarged rural markets and has further extended money economy, all of which is definite evidence of progress. It is equally true, however, that this increasing commercialisation of agriculture, under the present circumstances, has driven the peasants to take the risks of leaf prices which are more and more manipulated by the factories and collectors. The fortunes and indeed the very lives of the peasants have become absolutely dependent upon the tobacco market.

Yuan Chen-fu, a peasant from Yenan who knew Mao during the revolution.
One of the six hundred million Chinese who live and work on the land

CONTEMPORARY CHINA
The Revolution Continues

---

21 MAO'S REVOLUTIONARY FABLE

More than any other speech, document or article, the story of 'The Foolish Old Man who Moved the Mountains' sums up the spirit of the Chinese revolution. It was re-told by Mao Tse-tung in April 1945, close to the end of the struggle against Japan, not long before civil war broke out with the Kuomintang. Today in China it is learnt by children in their kindergartens to teach them dedication to the continuing revolutionary struggle, now directed to the harnessing of nature and the building of a socialist society. The original version of this story dates back to the fourth century BC when it was told by the philosopher Lieh Tzu. But the moral was added by Mao.

From *Mao Tse-tung's* Selected Works, *volume 3*

An old man lived in northern China long, long ago and was known as the Foolish Old Man of North Mountain. His house faced south and beyond his doorway stood the two great peaks, Taihang and Wangwu, obstructing the way. He called his sons, and hoe in hand they began to dig up these mountains with great determination.

Another greybeard, known as the Wise Old Man, saw them and said derisively, 'How silly of you to do this! It is quite impossible for you few to dig up these two huge mountains.' The Foolish Old Man replied, 'When I die, my sons will carry on; when they die, there will be my grandsons, and then their sons and grandsons, and so on to infinity. High as they are, the mountains cannot grow any higher and with every bit we dig, they will be that much lower. Why can't we clear them away?'

Having refuted the Wise Old Man's wrong view, he went on digging every day, unshaken in his conviction. God was moved by this, and he sent down two angels, who carried the mountains away on their backs.

Today, two big mountains lie like a dead weight on the Chinese people. One is imperialism, the other is feudalism. The Chinese Communist Party has long made up its mind to dig them up. We must persevere and work unceasingly, and we, too, will touch God's heart. Our God is none other than the masses of the Chinese people. If they stand up and dig together with us, why can't these two mountains be cleared away?

22 THE RED ARMY LEARNS SELF-RELIANCE

In 1927 Chiang Kai-shek launched a bloody purge against the Chinese Communists who were working with him and the Kuomintang to reunify China. In 1949 Chiang's Nationalist forces were annihilated by the Chinese Red Army and China was reunified by the Communists. In the two decades which came between, the Red Army and its leaders had experienced many epic adventures, won many heroic battles, expanding from a strength of a few tens of thousands after the Long March to no less than four million by the time of Liberation in 1949. But the greater part of this struggle was much less dramatic than the highlights of the Long March, the guerrilla war against Japan and the civil war with Chiang Kai-shek. It was often simply a struggle for the basic necessities of life, food, clothing and medicine. A warlord army could have robbed and plundered; a communist army, so Mao said, had to move among the people 'like fish in water'. If the people were alienated, the 'water' would evaporate. The Red armymen, bound by strict discipline not to take a grain of rice or a thread of cotton without payment, learnt how to 'rely on one's own resources' and to 'practise self-reliance'. (These two revolutionary concepts have since been applied on a much larger scale to whole areas of Chinese economic development since the Revolution.) The following story describes how the Red Army, in the remote mountains of northern Shensi province where their wartime capital of Yenan was established after the Long March, went foraging for medicinal herbs and practised 'self-reliance' in a small but vital way.

From an eyewitness account of the Long March by Fan Tse-ai

When the Red Army first arrived in northern Shensi at the end of the Long March, many of our comrades from southern China became ill. They were unaccustomed to the climate, and fell sick, mostly with influenza, diarrhoea and relapsing fever. The wards at the disposal of the Department of Health were filled to capacity. The Central Committee of the Party wanted the Red Army to take a rest before crossing the Yellow River on the east on their way to fight the Japanese invaders. This would provide an opportunity for the sick and wounded to recuperate as quickly as possible. Unfortunately our medical supplies had run out during the course of the Long March. Northern Shensi was far off the trading routes and Western medicines were unavailable in the local market. Because of the lack of surgical and medical supplies, it was impossible to perform even simple surgeries like tonsillectomy, let alone the treatment of chronic diseases. I remember an occasion when the chief of a divisional security section had tuberculosis of the lungs. Only after we had pleaded three times with the Department of Health, were we authorised to receive two bottles of cod-liver oil for him. That was a lot considering that the department had only four on hand.

As a matter of fact Dr Hu and a few other physicians had tried every possible substitute. Salt was used instead of the more usual disinfectants. Cotton quilts and bed-sheets, donated by the cadres, were boiled for use as surgical dressings. Wool was used for making swabs. But we found no way of overcoming the shortage of medicines. . . .

One afternoon, the comrades of the general service and the security squad of the Health Department were called to a meeting. It was an unusual kind of meeting, the political instructor talked about the shortages of medicines and the condition of our patients. Then Dr Hu rose to speak, holding some pieces of bark and roots in his hands. He described liquorice and white Chinese box-thorn, and showed us how to distinguish them by their roots and leaves. We realised that the purpose of the meeting was to urge us to go to the mountains and dig medicinal herbs for our sick and wounded comrades. It was an excellent idea and everyone got excited and wanted to get on with the job. An order to engage the enemy would not have met with a quicker response. . . .

There were wild animals in the forests. Sometimes, when we were bent over digging, a reindeer or a mountain goat darted out from

'New Year's Thanks to the Army'. A 1950 poster showing harmonious relations between the army and the people

behind us, and we would chase after it. But when packs of wolves or boars came along, we shouted at the top of our voices to scare them away. It would be a breach of discipline to waste a bullet on them. Dr Hu organised us into teams, each headed by a senior comrade as protection against wild beasts. However, the wild animals had their uses. One day we discovered something resembling a dried tree branch, which turned out to be antlers of great medicinal value. It was a prize discovery in those difficult days. Dr Hu was pleased beyond words.

When the snow came, the mountains were magnificent. The snowy peaks scintillated in the sun. The huge trees, coated by a thick layer of snow, looked like curling white dragons. The thawing snow was frozen into countless fantastic icicles. The snow blocked the paths and covered up the herbs, but we went up to the mountains as usual. An old villager who had tended sheep more than forty years heard about our activities in the mountains, and volunteered to be our guide. At that time, none of us had warm cotton-padded shoes. Many of us, the southerners, were still wearing straw sandals wrapped in a piece of goatskin. This queer foot-gear left enormous prints in the snow, and some people who did not know about our activities might think that strange animals had suddenly appeared in the mountains.

Sometimes we went deep into the woods, and it would be quite dark before we arrived home with our collection. We used to make a torch out of a tree branch by attaching to it bits of sulphur picked up in the mountains. It burned very well. In twos and threes, we would emerge from the mountains and the woods, hopping along and singing the songs of the mountain folk, as if we were enjoying a lantern festival. As we sang with increasing fervour, we forgot all about cold and fatigue.

During the day, when other comrades attended drills Dr Hu and I would prepare the tonic from the herbs. I tended the fire while he mixed the ingredients in the correct proportion, to ensure that the tonic was the correct consistency and the right temperature. The villagers used to call our billet 'the drug factory', but all we had at the 'factory' was three large cooking pots, and even these were borrowed from the villagers. Our fuel was firewood collected from the mountains.

In the evening, the cave, our billet, was turned into a busy laboratory. Dr Hu would take off his linen-faced overcoat and sit at the square table where he assembled many jars, each holding a specific kind of herb. By the light of a lantern, he mixed the herbs according to prescribed proportions. I helped in the minor work, such as crushing the herbs in a mortar. When the bugle sounded at bedtime, the doctor always told me to go to sleep but he kept on working late into the night. Next morning, the medicated paste would be all ready for making pills. We did not have the usual pill-making apparatus used in the drug stores, and rubbed out the pills one by one between our fingers. We youngsters found this most boring, and much preferred going up the mountains to gather the herbs.

We were billeted in Linchen Village over a month, during which we collected plenty of herbs and made a variety of medicines. I could name forty to fifty of them. Once out of curiosity I opened the medicine chest without the permission of the man in charge. I was delighted to find that two-thirds of the pills had been made by ourselves from the herbs gathered in the mountains. These pills proved to be good for the curing of colds, diarrhoea and other diseases. It was not long before most of the sick and wounded recovered and returned to their units.

23 PAPER TIGERS AND MAO'S VIEW OF THE WORLD

In August 1946, when Mao Tse-tung first spoke of 'paper tigers' in a conversation with the American journalist Anna Louise Strong, some of his colleagues took a gloomy view of the future. Chiang Kai-shek's Nationalist forces were on the offensive – in six months' time they would even capture the communist capital of Yenan. The United States, with little hesitation, was beginning to support Chiang with millions of dollars of economic and military aid (over 3000 millions by the end of the civil war). The Russians were pre-occupied with the cold war in Europe; Stalin had advised Mao to avoid civil war and to reach a political settlement with Chiang. Mao's view of the world, illustrated on this occasion 'with tea-cups and little wine-cups' on a table outside his Yenan cave-dwelling, is essentially the same optimistic view which he has held ever since.

The real struggle, even in the United States, is between the 'reactionaries' and the 'people', and it is the reactionaries who are 'paper tigers' along with all their nuclear weapons. Of course weapons are not unimportant but the people are the decisive factor. In saying that the talk of a war between the USA and the Soviet Union was a 'smokescreen' under cover of which the Americans were expanding their influence elsewhere (e.g. in China) Mao was contradicting the official Russian view that they were directly threatened. The effect of Mao's analysis then, and subsequently in Chinese foreign policy, is to attach much more importance to the popular 'struggle against imperialism' in the capitalist countries and their dependencies (including China at that time) in the Third World, than to the mainly great-power struggle between the United States and the Soviet Union. Mao's 'world view' also reflects an unshakeable confidence in the ability of a popular revolutionary movement to defeat, in the long run, the forces of reaction at home even if they are backed by foreign imperialism.

From the original version of Mao's talk with Anne Louise Strong, August 1946.

Like everyone else in Yenan, Chairman Mao lives in a cave. He lives, to be exact, in four caves opening on a terrace on the side of a hill. His dwelling is part of a cluster of perhaps a hundred caves along this hill-slope. I shall not tell precisely which hill-slope, for last week eight American-made planes bombed and strafed Yenan, and the bombs hit close to the cave where Mao had lived till a month ago. Yenan folk think those bombs were aimed at 'The Chairman'. But Mao had moved to another cave.

We sat on the flat clay terrace in front of his four-cave dwelling, watching the sunset fade on the arid, untamed hills. Around and below us grew Mao's garden, tall stalks of corn, big red tomatoes and some peanuts from which Mrs Mao had served us a delicious meal. Mao's small daughter played around her father's knees, climbed to his lap and then came over to investigate the foreign visitor, her shyness overcome by her curiosity. Looking up at the top of the cave I saw some fifty feet above us, children of the family of the upper ledge peering down through tall grasses to watch this funny foreign woman visiting the Chairman.

The Chairman talked about the civil war but preferred to talk world politics. In fact, he preferred interviewing me to letting me

The Date Garden near Yenan, where the communist leaders lived and planned the civil war, now a revolutionary memorial

interview him. He wanted to know anything I could tell him about America – politics, economics, labour movement, everything. When I asked what I could do for him, he said at once: 'Can you send in some recent American periodicals and books?' It is from visitors, from occasional books that pass the blockade, and from the tiny radio-receivers in the caves that listen in on outside news-services, that this isolated leader and philosopher must understand the world. . . .

Chairman Mao discussed Russo-American relations, illustrating them with tea-cups and little wine-cups placed on a table. He said that the talk of war between America and the USSR was, from the point of view of the present, only a smoke-screen which American reactionaries blow up to hide the more immediate antagonisms, namely those between American reactionaries and the American people and between the United States and the rest of the capitalist world.

'See, here are the American reactionaries,' he placed a big cup on one side of the table. 'And around them are first the American people' – a ring of little white earthenware wine-cups was placed around the big cup. 'Now here is the USSR' – tea-cup on the other side of the table.

'Between the USSR and America are all the other capitalist nations!' . . . These were marked by a long line of cups of all sizes. Mao laughed as he placed them, with the matches and cigarette packages crowded between.

'Now how can the American reactionaries fight with the Soviet Union? First of all, they have to attack the American people. Already the American reactionaries attack the American people. They oppress American workers and democratic elements politically and economically.

'To instigate war, the American reactionaries would have to attack the American people very much harder. They are preparing to introduce fascism in America. The American people should resist these reactionaries. I believe they will do so.'

'Now suppose the reactionaries get past the American people. Next come the other capitalist countries of the world. The American big capitalists are using anti-Russian fear as a pretext to bring the rest of the capitalist countries under American control. The trick of the American reactionaries is very much like that of the Japanese imperialists. They used the same pretext in China to cover attacks on the Chinese people.

'Here in the Pacific, America now controls more than all the former British sphere of influence. America controls Japan, China, half of Korea, and the South Pacific. She has long ago controlled Central and South America and thinks of controlling the whole of the British Empire and Western Europe. This is not at all pleasant to these countries and the broad masses of their people.

'Now all these naval bases and air bases that America has set up or is preparing to set up all over the world and that people say are against the USSR. It is quite true that they can be used against the USSR. But at present the first people oppressed by them are not the Russians but the people of all the other capitalist countries.

'America uses her finance capital to control England and other capitalist countries. She uses commerce to bring pressure upon the economic fabric of all capitalist countries.

'Before long England will consider who is it that is really oppressing her. Is it the USSR or is it America? Bevin's policy of uniting with America against Russia will meet with opposition from the English people. The American reactionaries will one day find themselves opposed by peoples of the whole world.'

'You speak of the talk of war between America and the USSR as a smoke-screen. Do you mean that such a war will not occur?' I asked.

'I do not say that American reactionaries do not want to fight the Soviet Union,' Mao retorted. 'They want to do so. They dream of wiping out the socialist country. American reactionaries think of ruling the entire world, including the USSR. The USSR is a powerful factor blocking them in their bid for world domination. That is why American reactionaries hate the USSR extremely. But people cannot but suspect their purpose when, just now, when World War Number Two has not been long concluded, they lay so much stress on war between the USSR and America and create a war atmosphere. Everyone knows that if America wants to fight the USSR she must do this through Great Britain, France, and China. That means, American reactionaries plan first of all to subjugate these countries and make them dependent countries or American colonies.

'Under such conditions will the masses of the people of these countries wait to be subjugated? Certainly not. They will rise and resist. I believe that, under the oppression of American imperialism, the American people should unite with the people of all capitalist countries against the attacks of American imperialism and its running-dogs in these countries. Only the victory of such a struggle can avert World War Number Three. Otherwise World War Number

Three is inevitable.'

'How do you like my theory?' smiled Mao, who is not a bit dogmantic and likes to discuss.

'What about the atomic bomb?' I replied. 'From their bases in Iceland, Okinawa, and China, can't the Americans bomb any city in Russia?'

'The atomic bomb,' said Mao, 'is a paper tiger. . . . Terrible to look at but not so strong as it seems. In the long view, real power belongs not to the reactionaries but to the people.'

Mao took a personal interest in seeing that I understood exactly what a paper tiger was. Lu Ting-yi, who translated for us, spoke at first of a 'scarecrow'. Mao stopped him and wanted to know what scarecrows were used for. A 'paper tiger' is a ferocious-looking creature that scares not crows but people, but that is really only made of pressed paper. After deciding that we would use the words 'paper tiger' instead of 'scarecrow', Mao kept repeating 'paper tiger', laughing at his own accent in English, throughout the following remarks.

'All reactionaries are paper tigers. . . . Before the February Revolution in 1917 in Russia, who had real power? Outwardly the Tsar had power. But what was this so-called power? A blast of the February Revolution blew the Tsar away. Ultimately power belonged to the Soviets of workers, soldiers and peasants. The Tsar was only a paper tiger!

'Was not Hitler regarded by people as very powerful? But history has shown him to be a paper tiger. Mussolini was the same. Imperialist Japan was the same. . . .'

We discussed various 'paper tigers', to each of which Mao tied the epithet in English, laughing at the unaccustomed sounds. 'Chiang Kai-shek – paper tiger,' he said.

'Wait a moment,' I halted him. 'Remembering that I am a correspondent. Do I write in the papers that Chairman Mao called Chiang a paper tiger?'

'Not just in those words,' laughed Mao. 'You must give the whole discussion. If Chiang supports the interests of the people, he is iron. If he deserts the people and launches war against them, he is a paper tiger. Precisely the latter is what Chiang has been doing.

'The American reactionaries are those paper tigers. People seem to think that they are very, very strong. The Chinese reactionaries use this "power" of the American reactionaries to frighten the Chinese. Like all reactionaries in history, they also will be proved to have no enduring strength. It is the American people that are strong, that have lasting power.' . . .

During the long talk night had fallen and we moved indoors from the terrace, for the summer nights are cold on Yenan's hills. Candles were brought, for Mao's dwelling furnishes no electric light for his long nights of work. By candlelight I made out the high white-washed arch of the cave and the stone flags of the floor. We talked over fresh teacups till Mrs Mao, in the adjoining cave, had put the small daughter to bed.

Then Chairman Mao and his wife accompanied me down the hill-side, with a kerosene lantern to show the uneven, winding path. We came to a wider but still uneven road where an auto-truck waited. Goodbyes were said. They stood on the hill-side watching as my truck jolted downwards and splashed into the rough bed of Yen River. Bright, very bright were the stars shining over the wild, dark Yenan hills.

24 THE PEASANTS STAND UP: LAND REFORM AND 'STRUGGLE'

Land reform under the communists was much more than a simple process of dividing up the landlords' estates among the poor. It was literally a 'struggle' in which the peasants were encouraged to 'stand up', to overcome their instinctive feelings of deference and dependence and to assert themselves against those who had op-pressed them in the past. Communist officials from outside set the struggle going, but its success depended upon the local leaders and rank and file of the peasant organisations. The redistribution of land started during the civil war (1946-9) in areas under communist control, where it also helped generate enthusiasm among peasants to join the People's Liberation Army in the greater 'struggle' against the Nationalists. After victory – the Liberation – in 1949 the land reform movement spread throughout the country.

The novelist Ting Ling joined a land reform work team in North China while the civil war was still being fought. Later she wrote her experiences into a best-selling novel, *The Sun Shines over the*

Sangkan River. In this extract the local bad guy, Schemer Chien, described as 'chief of the village racketeers', is at last brought before the masses. At first they hesitate to denounce him; Chien has good connections and his son-in-law is the village security officer. One of his sons (Yi) has also joined the Liberation Army. But once the dam of resentment against Chien is broken, the local leaders (Yumin and Tung) have to move fast in order to obey Communist Party instructions and save Schemer Chien from being lynched on the spot.

From chapter 50 of The Sun Shines over the Sangkan River

All this time Chien, standing on the stage gnawing his lips, was glancing round, wanting to quell these yokels, unwilling to admit defeat. For a moment he really had the mastery. He and his many years of power had become so firmly established in the village it was difficult for anyone to dislodge him. People hated him, and they had just been cursing him; but now that he stood before them they held their breath and faltered. It was like the pause before two game cocks start fighting, each estimating the other's strength. The longer the silence lasted the greater Chien's power became, until it looked as if he were going to win.

At this point a man suddenly leapt out from the crowd. He had thick eyebrows and sparkling eyes. Rushing up to Chien he cursed him: 'You murderer! You trampled our village under your feet! You killed people from behind the scenes for money. Today we're going to settle all old scores, and do a thorough job of it. Do you hear that? Do you still want to frighten people? It's no use! There's no place for you to stand on this stage! Kneel down! Kneel to all the villagers!' He pushed Chien hard, while the crowd echoed: 'Kneel down! Kneel down!' The militiamen held him, so that he knelt down properly.

Then the masses' rage swelled, they tasted power and their indignation waxed. A child's voice was heard: 'Put on the hat! Make him wear the hat!'

Fukuei jumped forward and asked: 'Who'll put it on? Whoever'll put it on, come up here!'

While the crowd was shouting 'Make him wear the hat! Put on the hat!' a boy of thirteen or fourteen jumped up, lifted the hat and set it on Chien's head, at the same time spitting at him and cursing: 'Here you are, Chien!' Then he jumped down, while people laughed.

By now Chien had lowered his head completely, his malevolent

Storming the heights of feudalism. A wartime woodcut from Yenan

eyes could no longer sweep their faces. The tall paper hat made him look like a clown. Bent basely from the waist, screwing up his eyes, he had lost all his power, had become the people's prisoner, a criminal against the masses.

The man who had cursed Chien turned now to face the crowd, and they all saw that it was Cheng, the Chairman of the Peasants' Association.

'Friends!' said Cheng. 'Look at him and me, look how pampered he is; it's not cold yet but he's wearing a lined gown. Then look at me, look at yourselves. Do we look like human beings! Hah, when our mothers bore us, we were all alike! We've poured our blood and sweat to feed him. He's been living on our blood and sweat, oppressing us all these years; but today we want him to give back money for money, life for life, isn't that right?'

'Right! Give back money for money, life for life!' . . .

Then people rushed up to the stage, stumbling over each other to confront Chien. Chien's wife with tear-stained cheeks stood behind her husband, pleading with them all: 'Good people, have pity on my old man! Good people!' Her hair was dishevelled, there were no longer flowers in it, the traces of black varnish could still be seen. She was just like a female clown in the theatre, making a fine couple with her husband. She had echoed him all her life, and now she still clung to him, unwilling to separate their fates.

One accusation was brought after another. Liuman kept leading the crowd to shout slogans. Some peasants were so carried away that they climbed onto the stage and struck at Chien as they questioned him, while the crowd backed them up: 'Beat him, beat him to death!'

Chien was helpless. Trying to extricate himself, he said: 'Good people, I was guilty of everything. I admit it all, whether I did it or not. I only ask you to be generous!'

His wife too said tearfully: 'For the sake of our son in the Eighth Route Army, be merciful to him!'

'Damn it!' Liuman jumped up. 'Have I wronged you! Say, did you trick my father into starting that mill or not?'

'Yes, I did,' Chien had to admit.

'Did you have my eldest brother conscripted or not!'

'Yes, I did.'

'Did you drive my second brother mad, or not?'

'Yes, yes.'

'Have I condemned you wrongly?'

The peasants stand up. Denouncing the local 'tyrant'

'No.'

'Damn it! Then why should you say "whether I did it or not". Let's ask him what injustice there's been! Damn him, what does he want us to take him for! Let me tell you, I'm going to thrash this out with you: you give me back my father, give me back my eldest brother. Give me back my second brother!'

'Let him pay with his life!' someone shouted. 'Kill him!'

People surged up to the stage, shouting wildly: 'Kill him!' 'A life for our lives!'

A group of villagers rushed to beat him. It was not clear who started, but one struck the first blow and the others fought to get at him, while those behind who could not reach him shouted:

'Throw him down! Throw him down! Let's all beat him!'

One feeling animated them all – vengeance! They wanted vengeance! They wanted to give vent to their hatred, the sufferings of the oppressed since their ancestors' times, the hatred and loathing of thousands of years; all this resentment they directed against him. They would have liked to tear him with their teeth.

The cadres could not stop everyone jumping onto the stage. With blows and curses the crowd succeeded in dragging him down from the stage and then more people swarmed towards him. Some crawled over across the heads and shoulders of those in front.

Chien's silk gown was torn. His shoes had fallen off, the white paper hat had been trampled into pieces underfoot. All semblance of order was gone and Chien was going to be beaten to death, when Yumin remembered Pin's last instructions and pushed his way into the crowd. [Pin is a Party official from the County authorities.] Having no other way of stopping them, he shielded Chien with his body, and shouted: 'Don't be in such a hurry to beat him to death! We've got to ask the county authorities!' And then the militiamen hastily checked the people. . . .

Old Tung stepped forward and addressed the crowd: 'Chien owes you money and lives. Just killing him won't make it up to you, will it?'

'If he died several deaths he couldn't make it up,' someone said.

'Well, look,' said Old Tung, 'can he take any more beating?'

By this time Chien had already been carried back onto the stage. He lay there panting like a dying dog, and someone said: 'Kill the dog.'

'Bah! Killing's too good for him. Let's make him beg for death. Let's humble him for a few days, how about it?' Old Tung's face was red with excitement. He had started life as a hired labourer. Now that he saw peasants just like himself daring to speak out and act boldly his heart was racing wildly with happiness.

'Right,' someone agreed.

'If you don't pull the roots a weed will always make trouble,' another said.

'Why are you afraid of him? Don't be afraid. As long as we're united like today we can keep him in order. Think of a way to deal with him.'

'Yes, I've a proposal. Let's have the whole village spit at him, what about that?'

'I say his property should be divided up among us all.'

'Make him write a statement, admitting his crimes, and if he opposes us again, we'll have his life.'

'Yes, let him write a statement. Make him write it himself.'

Here Chien raised himself again and kneeled to kotow to the crowd. His right eye was swollen after his beating so that the eye looked even smaller. His lip was split and mud was mixed with the blood. His bedraggled moustaches drooped disconsolately. He was a fearful sight, and as he thanked the villagers his voice was no longer clear and strong, but he stammered out: 'Good people! I'm kowtowing to you good folks. I was quite wrong in the past. Thank you for your mercy. . . .'

A group of children softly aped his voice: 'Good people! . . .'

Then he was dragged over to write a statement. He was in a half numbed state, but he had to take the brush in his trembling hand and write line by line. Then everyone discussed the question of confiscating his property and decided to appropriate all, including that of Chienli [one of Chien's sons]. But they could not touch Yi's twenty-five *mou*. The peasants were dissatisfied, but this was an order from above, because Yi [another son] was a soldier in the Eighth Route Army! So they had to put up with it.

By now the sun was sinking. Some of the children were kicking pebbles for hunger at the back of the meeting, and some of the women went quietly home to prepare a meal. The presidium urged Chien to hurry up and finish writing, saying everybody was tired of waiting for him, and asking where his usual ability had gone to.

When the chairman started reading the statement the crowd grew tense again, and shouted, 'Make him read it himself!'

Chien knelt in the middle of the stage, his lined gown hanging in shreds, shoeless, not daring to meet anyone's eyes. He read: 'In the past I committed crimes in the village, oppressing good people . . . !'

'That won't do! Just to write "I" won't do! Write "local despot, Chien".'

'Yes, write "I, the local despot, Chien".'

'Start again!'

Then Chien started reading again: 'I, Chien, a local despot, committed crimes in the village, oppressing good people, and I deserve to die a hundred times over; but my good friends are merciful . . .'

'Who the devil are you calling your good friends?' An old man rushed forward and spat at him.

'Go on reading! Just say all the people of the village.'

'No, why should he call us his people.'

'Say all the gentlemen.'

'Say all the poor gentlemen. We don't want to be rich gentlemen! Only the rich are called gentlemen.'

Chien had to continue: 'Thanks to the mercy of all the poor gentlemen in the village . . .'

'That's no good. Don't say poor gentlemen; today we poor people have stood up. Say "the liberated gentlemen", and it can't be wrong.'

'Thanks to the mercy of the liberated gentlemen, my unworthy life has been spared . . .'

'What! I don't understand.' Another voice from the crowd interrupted Chien. 'We liberated gentlemen aren't going to pass all this literary stuff. Just put it briefly; say your dog's life has been spared.'

'Yes, spare your dog's life!' the rest agreed.

Chien had to go on: 'Spare my dog's life. In future I must completely change my former evil ways. If I transgress in the slightest or oppose the masses, I shall be put to death. This statement is made by the local despot Chien, and signed in the presence of the masses. 3 August.'

The presidium asked the crowd to discuss it, but very few further amendments were proposed, although a few people still felt he was getting off too lightly and they ought to beat him some more.

Chien was allowed to go back. He was only permitted to live in Yi's house for the time being. All his property apart from his land was to be straightway sealed up by the Peasants' Association. As to the question of how much should be left him, that was left to the Land Division Committee to decide.

25 THE PURGE OF THE SNAILS

Schistosomiasis is a widespread debilitating disease which is found in the tropics and sub-tropics of Africa, south-western and eastern Asia and Latin America. The schistosome or parasitic blood fluke is transmitted to man by water-dwelling snails; ironically the snails flourish in the very irrigation systems which are essential for peasant agriculture. The eggs and worms of the fluke have even been identified in Egyptian mummies dating back thousands of years. With the rapid expansion of rural medical services in China since 1949 the disease has been brought under control although it has still not been totally eliminated. But it is probably more successfully contained in China than in any other developing country afflicted by it. The following extract describes in detail how the disease was tackled in the mid-1950s in part of the Yangtze province of Kiangsu. Note how the medical workers had to contend not only with the disease itself but with the reluctance to co-operate of the local peasants who regarded it fatalistically as part of their natural lot. To fight this and other diseases required a new form of mass 'struggle' in the countryside.

From China Reconstructs, *August 1957*

> In the Chinghsi (Blue River) fat perches swim.
> Along its banks rice-flowers bloom.

This is what the peasants of Chingpu county on the banks of the Tayingkiang River in southern Kiangsu province once sang of their rich homeland. But for the past few decades, the words of the song had been altered to:

> By the Chinghsi widows weep,
> And the land lies desolate.

Ask any peasant the reason for the desolation, and he will tell you 'big belly'.

The medical term for 'big belly' is schistosomiasis. This disease has been a curse not only in Chingpu but to wide areas of China, along and south of the Yangtze and its myriad of contributing lakes, rivers and canals in eleven provinces.

According to an investigation, in 1955 about 10,407,000 people in

China were affected. An illustration of its disastrous character can be found in the history of Jentun village in Kiangsu province. Since the disease first appeared there in 1930, 80 of the original 244 families have been completely wiped out. In each of 28 other families, only one person was living in 1951. At that time 97 per cent of the remaining villagers suffered from it.

In 1955, over 50 per cent of Chingpu county's 270,000 people had schistosomiasis. By 1957, about 10 per cent of the cases had been successfully treated, and it was well on the way to being stamped out. Chingpu is one of the pilot projects in the nation-wide campaign to wipe out schistosomiasis, and what was done there in the past few years is now being applied all over the affected area. By the end of 1957 1,700,000 cases will have been treated, 1,100,000 this year alone, and the groundwork will be laid to eradicate the disease in seven years.

Schistosomiasis is caused by schistosomes or blood flukes, a genus of parasites prevalent in wide areas of the globe. The one found most commonly in China is *Schistosoma japonicum*, which enters the blood stream through the skin and lays its eggs there. These excrete a kind of toxin which destroys human tissue. The results are emaciation, distension of the abdomen, listlessness and, in the later stages, complete inability to work. Women cannot conceive; children's growth is stunted. The chronic stage may be prolonged for several years or the patients may die from pneumonia or other illnesses which they contract because of low resistance.

The schistosomes spread chiefly through lack of proper sanitation. When the eggs which are evacuated with the faeces reach fresh water, they hatch, and the miracidia, or microscopic larvae, enter the shells of tiny snails (*Oncomelania*) which inhabit slow-flowing rivers, ponds or paddy-fields. Growing into cercariae or full-grown schistosomes, they bore beneath the skin of people bathing or washing clothes in the infected water, or working in flooded fields.

In the old days, it was the custom in the country to store night-soil [human excreta] in large jars on the riverbanks to be used later as fertiliser, and to rinse the chamber-pots in the river. Chinpu county alone is criss-crossed by more than 3500 winding rivers and many other irrigation ditches, which are the perfect breeding-place for the schistosomes and the snails which harbour them. But now the 'schistosomiasis belt' has eighteen special medical centres, 240 stations and over 1000 medical teams – a total staff of over 23,000 to combat the disease. Studying and testing new methods of pre-

A doctor practising traditional Chinese medicine in a Shanghai clinic. Note the acupuncture charts on the walls.

vention and treatment are sixty-seven medical colleges and other research institutes.

Since the Chingpu county anti-schistosomiasis station was set up in June 1951 its staff has grown to a hundred, including sixteen doctors of western medicine and two traditional Chinese practitioners, as well as eighteen members engaged in preventive work. On the nursing staff of twenty, five are trained nurses, while the others are primary and junior middle-school graduates and demobilised army men who received a special intensive course in the work at two large anti-schistosomiasis centres at Sung-kiang and Wusih, in Kiangsu.

The station is bustling now, but the handful who opened it did not find a warm reception during the first years. They found that one of the first needs was to win the confidence of the peasants. The latter did not know how the illness was spread, but blamed their 'bad locality and terrain'. Some attributed it to the crimes of their ancestors, for which the present generation was having to pay. In the early stages of the illness, since the affected person could still carry on his work more or less as usual, most were reluctant to undergo treatment. The peasants, who were farming individually at that time, were unwilling to leave their work for the necessary month's stay at the hospital.

Deciding to launch a public-education campaign and make one of the *hsiangs*[1] in the county a demonstration spot, in 1954 the staff put up posters and went from door to door with their microscopes, showing the peasants the eggs and larvae and explaining their effect. That 'big belly' was caused by tiny worms which could not even be seen by the naked eye was indeed impressive, the peasants granted. But if the gods and spirits had not been able to cure it, they asked, how could the city doctors do so? After much persuasion, in spring 1955, twenty-two very hesitant patients, bringing with them their own rice, bedding and bed-planks, moved into the rooms of the *hsiang* government's office which had been set aside as a 'demonstration' hospital.

They were treated with tartar emetic, the crystalline white salt which since 1918 has been the main western medicine effective in killing the schistosomes. Patients received slow intravenous injections of one per cent solution once a day for twenty days. Although

[1]An administrative district.

they experienced the usual reactions of nausea and diarrhoea, most were not completely bedridden. The 'pioneer' patients, many of whom were primary-school students, found the medical workers good friends. During the nightly story-telling and social hour, they made up ditties together about the illness and its cure, which the patients could sing to their friends on their return home. In all, they remained in the hospital a month for treatment and a time of rest and observation. The results were typical: 60 per cent were pronounced cured, while 40 per cent, most of whom were in an advanced stage, were improved but were warned of possible relapse.

By late 1955, the whole *hsiang* was ready to undertake the campaign on a mass scale. In the spring of that year, most of the peasants in the *hsiang* had organised into thirteen agricultural producers' co-operatives. This was a great boon to the project, for it provided an organisational base on which to begin the work.

The preventive campaign consisted of three steps: disposing of the night-soil in a hygienic manner, ensuring the purity of the water in the rivers, and destroying the snails in which the blood flukes made their homes. All 488 of the night-soil jars were moved from the river-banks. A system was devised so that when each jar was full, it would be sealed with lime paste for the storage period. This, plus the tight cover, prevented the contents from losing their natural ammonia, which acted as a disinfectant, killing the schistosome eggs within a few days. So treated, the night-soil could be applied to the ground as fertiliser without further contaminating the waters. Washing of chamber-pots in the river was strictly forbidden, and instead tanks were provided.

An investigation revealed that the snails averaged ten to twenty per square foot along the river-banks. In autumn 1955, when the amphibian snails came near the banks to spend the winter, the movement to wipe them out got under way. The station's preventive team taught sixty peasants to spray the banks and surrounding lowlands with calcium arsenate to kill them. Paddy-fields in which the snails were embedded were temporarily drained to permit teams to work on them. Another method, which has been practised widely by the Japanese, was to bury the snails. In January of 1956, when farm work was at a lull, most of the *hsiang*'s residents engaged in a three-day mobilisation for this. They took off the topsoil which was infested by the snails and buried this earth in deep ditches, in which the snails would suffocate. Used on a smaller scale was a system invented by workers in the Wusih anti-schistosomiasis centre. The snails in the weeds near the banks were sprayed with burning hydrogen and carbon monoxide. This method proved over 90 per cent effective. It is estimated that during the mobilisation, 80 per cent of the snails in the *hsiang* were exterminated, and the rest will meet their doom before the end of this year. In the whole country, snails were eliminated from an estimated 93 square miles in 1956.

26 REVOLUTION AMONG THE NON-CHINESE CHINESE

More than sixty per cent of Chinese territory is the homeland of the 'national minorities', those who are not of Chinese or 'Han' nationality. In numbers they make up about a twelfth of the Chinese population. At the time of Liberation a few of these fifty or so minorities were still living outside the control of any central government; many were slave or feudal societies. The following article, written by two Chinese anthropologists in 1957, describes some of the attempts to bring these minorities forward towards socialism while preserving their distinctive identities. The authors discuss China's largest national minority, the by now five million Uighurs in Sinkiang on the borders of Soviet Kazakhstan; other large minorities (which they do not discuss here) are to be found in Inner Mongolia and Tibet. Chinese policy in these large border regions, complicated by relations with the Soviet Union and India, has not always been easy to follow. The Chinese themselves have admitted to mistakes being made under the influence of what they call 'Great-Han chauvinism'. It is particularly difficult to learn much about the situation in Tibet since the uprising of 1959. But it is worth remembering that in Tibet, as in many of the other societies described in this article, the great majority of the people were living in a state of feudal backwardness imposed upon them by the Buddhist lamas and nobility. In all these societies the Chinese Communists are faced with the same problem: how to promote necessary social reforms without destroying the minority's national culture and identity.

A paper-cut illustration of peasant women wearing the distinctive costume of a national minority

From an article by Fei Hsiao-tung and Lin Yueh-hwa, China Reconstructs, *April 1957*

There are more than fifty minority nationalities in China, embracing about 35 million people all told. Because they were oppressed for so long, many of them remained technically and educationally backward. Some, at the time of liberation, were still living in tribes and clans – in a primitive communist society with common ownership. Some were in slave society. Some were at the feudal stage, with serfdom.

It is the firm intention of the People's Government that the minority peoples shall not be left behind in the advance to socialism that is transforming the whole nation. At the same time, change cannot be forced on them by the state or accomplished for them by the majority nationality – it must be carried out by the people themselves. And every effort must be exerted to see that it proceeds peacefully, without violence to the internal unity, traditions or religious beliefs of the nationality concerned. . . .

An example of primitive communism is found among the Olunchuns. The smallest of the country's nationalities, numbering only about 2200 people, they inhabit the forests of the Khingan Mountains in Northeast China. They are primarily hunters, living a migratory life and catching fish between hunting seasons. Each clan has its own communally-owned hunting and fishing grounds. The men do the hunting and the women the household work; marriage within the clan is not permitted. The men go out in small groups – for defence against wild beasts – and their kill is shared out equally, with a portion set aside for widows, orphans, and sick or disabled members of the clan.

Each clan or tribe decides its own affairs by common discussion. In cases of disputes, the elders are generally called on to give their ruling after a general debate with the parties concerned. Land is held in common. Firearms, horses, hunting dogs and household utensils are the private property of each family, though they are freely shared in case of necessity. Up till about 1920 the Olunchuns had scarcely any firearms, and hunted with bows and arrows. They then had little or no surplus to exchange for agricultural or other goods. But with the arrival of fur traders and the introduction of guns, they could kill more animals, and furs became an important commodity and source of wealth. Thereafter the meat was still divided, but the skin of each animal went to the hunter who killed it.

Rich and poor families began to appear within each clan, wealth being judged by the number of horses owned by each. But to this day no distinct class divisions exist among the Olunchun people. The use of private property to exploit the labour of others is unknown.

The first step the government took to help the Olunchun people forward was to give them local autonomy so that they could manage their own affairs. In 1951, the Olunchun Autonomous Banner[1] was established as part of the Inner Mongolian Autonomous Region. Then, working through the banner government, new and varied ways of making a livelihood were introduced among the hunters – agriculture, forestry and the herding of deer. The people were encouraged to build permanent settlements. Primary schools and health stations were set up. A many-sided economy is the path by which the Olunchun people will advance.

But, as might be expected, the process of building socialism on the basis of primitive society produces some surprises. Last year, for example, some thirty hunters' co-operatives were organised in the Olunchun Banner. These had obvious benefits – a better division of labour, collective trading arrangements and so on. But the organisers, thinking somewhat mechanically in terms of the usual practice of farm and other co-operatives, wished to stimulate the hunters' activity by fixing the distribution of the game strictly according to the work done by each. This seemed a strange step to the Olunchuns, accustomed to equal shares for all. Eventually there was a solution embodying both features – twenty to thirty per cent of the game was set aside for special awards to the best hunters, and the rest was divided equally as before. . . .

Slavery, the stage that follows that of primitive communism in the scale of social development, can also still be seen among some of China's minorities. The Yi people live in the south-western provinces of Szechuan, Yunnan and Kweichow. In the eighth century AD they were very prosperous and appear to have had their own state in Yunnan, together with some other nationalities there. Today they number over 3,250,000, of whom 860,000 live in the Liangshan Mountain area in Szechuan province.

Yi society has developed unevenly and varies from place to place. In Yunnan and Kweichow it has long been feudal, but in one part of the Liangshan Mountains a distinct slave system has persisted. The Yis there live by agriculture of a somewhat primitive kind, and

[1]An administrative division in Inner Mongolia corresponding to a county.

carry on other occupations – livestock breeding, weaving, iron-work and building. There is no clear division of labour between the farmer and the handicraft worker – the same person does both. They have no merchants and no market.

Everyone belongs to one of two main categories – Black and White. Those terms correspond roughly to two classes, masters and slaves. The Black Yis had slaves whom they could buy, sell or even put to death. They also owned most of the land, livestock, buildings and tools. They did little or no productive work, regarding labour as beneath them. They lived mainly on the wealth produced by their slaves, as well as rent (from another category of slaves who were closer to serfs) and usury.

The White Yis, largely the slave class, can further be classified according to their three kinds of relationship with the Black. The *Kashikalo* ('hearth-tenders') were unmarried people and were absolute chattels, performing household, farming, handicraft and other work for their masters and possessing no rights, property or tools of their own. Marrying with their owners' permission, they could become *Anchia* ('settled family slaves') and rent small plots of land for themselves. But they still were not permitted to move their homes and had to live near their masters so as to be at hand when required for work. Finally, on payment of a stipulated redemption fee, they could become *Chuno*, with a measure of personal freedom, private property and parental rights over their children. Even then, however, they depended on their masters for protection against being enslaved by others. Both *Chuno* and *Anchia* could own slaves in their turn, and these slaves might also own slaves. There were said to be instances of 'slaves of the seventh degree'.

Though he might move to a different level within his own category, a White Yi could never become a Black Yi. Marriage between the two was strictly prohibited. A Black Yi could sell, rob, torture or kill a White Yi and the latter had no redress. No Black Yi, whatever the circumstances, could be degraded to White.

Naturally, there was class conflict. It was quite common for slaves to destroy their masters' tools and implements and run away. But because the White Yis lived in scattered and hostile communities and were themselves divided into socially antagonistic groups, the slaves could never form a united force to overthrow their masters. This, with the ruthless national oppression from which both masters and slaves suffered in the past and the incessant blood feuds among the clans and tribes, was the principal cause of the long-standing impoverishment and backwardness of Yi society as a whole.

Among the Yis, the people's government began its work by trying to put an end, by reconciliation, to blood feuds and slave raiding. Reasoning and persuasion were used to convince leaders that the enmity between them had in fact been fomented by China's former rulers for their own ends – 'divide and rule'. Repeated negotiations were promoted to bring about peaceful settlement.

Then self-government organisations were built up region by region. In April 1952, the Yi Autonomous *Chou*[1] was set up in the Liangshan mountain area, embracing fourteen counties and over a million people, four-fifths of them Yis. In accordance with local conditions, peaceful negotiations with the chiefs led to the beginning of democratic reform. Last year more than 40,000 bond-slaves were freed with their masters' agreement. The *chou* government helped them to obtain their own houses, furniture and farm implements, and soon they will form agricultural co-operatives.

At liberation, a large number of China's national minorities were in stages of feudal society, each with its own special characteristics. The Uighur people constitute three-quarters of the population of Sinkiang (the huge province in China's far northwest, now the Sinkiang Uighur Autonomous Region). They had several different forms of feudal relationships. The feudal rulers in Moyu county in southern Sinkiang were known as *Hochia* (nobility). They owned big demesnes which they divided into two parts. One was the manor farm, tilled by their serfs without payment. The other was divided among the serfs, who could cultivate it when they were not doing unpaid labour for their masters. A *Hochia* could do what he liked with his serfs and their property. He kept his own court and prison, and could mete out corporal punishment, torture and even death to offenders. Serfs could be sold or given away.

This early kind of feudal serfdom, however, was already becoming rare. Much more common was a sort of combination of *corvée* (obligatory labour) and fifty-fifty sharing of crops, belonging to the middle stage of feudalism. In villages nearer to urban centres, the landlords engaged in commerce, extorted huge rents in kind from the people and employed wage-labourers. This is a later stage of feudalism, and had not developed to any great extent in Uighur society.

After 1949 the Uighurs carried out the land reform like the people elsewhere in China. The rule of the landlords was broken. More

[1]An administrative unit below the province.

than two million peasants got land of their own – or additional land where theirs had been insufficient. The co-operative movement followed. Autonomy was introduced by steps and on 1 October 1955 a number of autonomous units were combined together to form the Sinkiang Uighur Autonomous Region, the largest in China, with 3,737,000 Uighur people, a considerably smaller number belonging to several other nationalities. By September last year more than ninety per cent of all Sinkiang peasant households had joined agricultural producers' co-operatives. They are starting to develop livestock-breeding on a large scale. The time-table by which the Uighur people are entering socialism is roughly the same as that of the Hans (the majority people of China).

In south and southwest Yunnan province, not far from the Burma border, live the Tai people numbering about 470,000. At the time of liberation, the economy of the Tais of Hsishuangpanna in southern Yunnan was mainly feudal, with remnants of primitive society (they had probably skipped the stage of slavery). Several forms of land ownership existed side by side – communal, by the feudal lord (predominant), and by the peasant. The feudal lords were a kind of hereditary local official called *tu-ssu*, first created in the thirteenth century by the Chinese imperial court for the purpose of rule over vassal peoples. By this device, the old practice of equal distribution of land was turned into the equal distribution of obligation to the feudal lord. The village commune became the labour team through which the feudal lord exacted service from his serfs. The popular village council remained in existence, but lost its democratic content. Tai society stayed that way, feudal in substance though keeping some of its original communal form.

The Hsishuangpanna Tai Autonomous *Chou* was established in 1953. Two years later the democratic reform was begun. In accordance with the expressed wishes of the people, and with the assistance of government officials of their own nationality, the *tu-ssu* and local chieftains, to whom the nationality policy of the government had been carefully explained, relinquished their claim to tribute, rent and interest, the imposition of forced labour and other exploitation. After that, land reform was carried out peacefully by consultation with the landlords, it being the rule that they should get a share of land just as the peasants did. Their houses, farm implements and grain stocks were not confiscated, and their political rights and positions were retained. By the end of last year this process had been carried out smoothly.

27 LOVE IN A MOUNTAIN VILLAGE

It is a mild winter in Chinghsi, a village up in the hills in Hunan province. The local leadership, led by a woman Party official from the county town, is trying to whip up enthusiasm for establishing agricultural co-operatives, the next stage of land reform. But many peasants are reluctant to lose independent control of their newly won land. Ex-landlords and other 'bad elements' are spreading rumours that 'everything will be confiscated'. Some peasants rush up into the wooded mountain slopes to cut down their bamboos and timber in case these should be included in the co-operative.

Chen Ta-chun, commander of the local militia and secretary of the Youth League, is an impetuous young man, active in the struggle to set up co-operatives, and he has big plans for the future. Sheng Shu-chun, a girl with long eyelashes and large black eyes, would like to join Chen's Youth League although not just for political reasons. In this extract from the novel by Chou Li-po, Sheng's application is finally approved and she has a chance to talk with Chen alone. But are their minds on the same subject?

From the novel, Great Changes in a Mountain Village

At this point, Chen Ta-chun felt excited. He took Sheng Shu-chun's arm, left the sweet potato plot, took a narrow path across the hill, through trees so thick that they hid the sky, and said affectionately:

'Shu-chun, I want to tell you something. I have plans in my mind.'

'What kind of plans?'

'You must keep them secret, or I won't tell you.'

'I promise.'

'After the co-operative is established, I'm going to propose that we do away with all the ridges between the fields, and make small plots into large ones. With large fields, the Iron Buffalo can go into the water.'

'What Iron Buffalo?'

'Tractors. They don't get tired and can work the fields day and night. Then we would be able to grow two crops of rice in all the fields.'

'Even in dry fields?' Shu-chun was doubtful.

'We must plan to build a reservoir, look,' he pointed to a ravine in the hills opposite. 'Isn't that just the place for a reservoir? When we've built a reservoir, all the dry fields in the village will be irrigated, and even after paying tax we shan't be able to eat all the grain we grow. We'll send the surplus grain to help feed the workers in industry. Won't that be wonderful! Then they, all smiles, will come in their jeeps to the countryside, and say to us, "Hello, peasant-brothers, would you like to have electric light here?" "Yes, paraffin lamps are really too inconvenient and wasteful." "Very well, we'll install it. Do you want the telephone?" "Yes, we want that as well." And so, electric light and the telephone will come to the countryside.'

'You talk as if the electric light was just going to come on!'

'It'll be soon, we won't have to wait for ten or even five years. Then we'll use some of the co-operative's accumulated funds to buy a lorry and when you women go to the theatre in town, you can ride by lorry. With electric light, telephone, lorries and tractors, we shall live more comfortably than they do in the city, because we have the beautiful landscape and the fresh air. There'll be flowers all the year round and wild fruit, more than we can eat: chinquapins [dwarf chestnuts] and chestnuts all over the hills.'

'We can plant peach trees, pear trees and orange trees, too.'

'Of course, you can plant as many as you like. In front of and behind everybody's house, at the edge of ponds, around the reservoir, on the hills, we'll plant them everywhere. Within five years, you'll see, as soon as spring comes, there'll be pink peach-blossom, snow-white pear-blossom and delicate yellow orange-blossom, all over the villages, and the hills, the land and the dykes. They'll look like sunset clouds or brocade, and when our worker-brothers come down to the country, they'll feel as if they had missed the path and gone into someone's garden!'

Sheng Shu-chun was walking on his left side. She looked at his profile in the moonlight: his dark, healthy face had a shining and yet hazy, intoxicated look, as if the myriad-coloured flowery garden were there in front of his eyes. They walked on and he continued:

'When the fruit is ripe, and cadres and workers come down from the city, we'll hand them platefuls and say, "Try our local fruit, it's not bad. Not too sour? We're improving this breed now." '

As he talked, it was as if the visitors were really here, and were eating the fresh fruit that he had picked. Sheng Shu-chun laughed:

'Nothing but food; you haven't mentioned recreation. Where shall we have our club?'

Taking time off from a political lecture

'Girls think of nothing but the club! Don't worry, we'll build it. If you like, we'll elect you chairman. We must buy a few more packs of cards, Chairman Li is mad keen on cards. Just think, how happy we shall be then!'

'Must we wait till then before we can be happy?'

'It's not bad now, but we still have difficulties.'

'Don't tell me about your difficulties, I don't want to hear about them. I have something important to ask you. May I?'

'Go on.'

'Tell me. Suppose there is someone, like me. She, for instance. . . .' She hesitated, as if there was something she couldn't get out.

'She what?'

'Never mind. We won't talk about it. Let's go down, it's chilly up here'. Though she had spoken so clearly and obviously, he still didn't understand, or pretended not to understand. Once again she felt he was cold towards her.

'If you feel too cold here, I'll take you to a nice place.' For some reason Chen Ta-chun didn't want to leave her this evening and he threw his appointment with Sheng Ching-ming to the winds.

'Where are we going?' She followed him.

'There is a brick-kiln on the southern slope, it'll be warm there.'

When they got to the southern slope, they could see smoke rising from the brick-kiln chimney. Near by was a thatched wood-shed, facing south, and backing on the kiln. They went into the shed and it was very warm. They sat side by side on a bundle of faggots. The moon-beams slanted in from the west under the low straw eaves and shone directly on them. Shu-chun's face in this clear light looked unusually delicate, beautiful and alluring. Inside this isolated and silent wood-shed, her heart was pounding more than ever. Ta-chun, calm as usual, asked her:

'Didn't you say, you had something important to ask me? Now you can tell me what it is.'

His manner was still official, as if he had no personal feelings himself, and no inkling of Sheng Shu-chun's feelings. Actually, he had. But, in the first place, he was, as Li Yueh-hui said, 'walking on primrose paths,' as several girls in the village were in love with him. There was even one so daring that, copying the city fashion, she had written him a letter and expressed her feelings openly to him. Being in such an advantageous position naturally aroused his male pride and dignity, and he would not easily reveal the feelings buried at the bottom of his heart. In the second place, he and several friends of the same age had recently made a mutual plan not to allow themselves to fall in love, let alone marry, before they were twenty-eight. Why did they choose the age of twenty-eight and not thirty or twenty-five? Their calculation was, by the time they were twenty-eight, the state's Second Five-Year Plan would have been completed and tractors would be coming to Chinghsi Township. Then, how exciting it would be to look for a wife among the girls who would be driving tractors! . . .

One of the most beautiful girls in the township had made clear her intentions, and she was here in front of him, alone, on the hill, in this small hut full of firewood. No one could see them; there was only the clear and cold moonlight to keep them company. He knew this girl was sought after by many; both in looks and in ideas she was the most outstanding girl in the village. As for himself, to be honest, he liked to see her often, and when he saw her, his feelings became extraordinarily tender, and he always wanted to say a word or two, suitable for her, loving, gentle, and warm. But he was no good at this; as soon as he opened his mouth, his tongue slid on to his plans: tractors, lorries, small plots becoming large ones, and so forth, all dry and official. Sheng Shu-chun took every opportunity to entangle him; she was always trying to hold him in a net woven by her feminine, half-spoken, gentle and careful thoughts. At this moment, she said casually:

'Do you know, I have a friend who wants to see you?'

'Who? What for?'

'I won't tell you yet who it is. At any rate, it is somebody.' She deliberately teased him.

'Well, who is it? Has he got something important to see me about?' The responsible Ta-chun was beginning to feel anxious.

'You could call it extremely important, or you could call it unimportant. It depends who you're talking to.' She was still being difficult.

'You don't care about worrying people to death?'

'You do official work every day and yet you're still so impatient. Wouldn't it be better if you learned to be a little more steady and mature?'

'Who is it? Is it a man or woman?'

'I won't tell you her name yet, it's an inexperienced girl, rather like me, but not entirely. She wants to see you,' her words still came in little bursts, 'to make sure, if she. . . .' The girl hesitated and looked down.

'If she what?' Observing her embarrassed manner Chen Ta-chun had guessed part of the truth, but still pretended not to have noticed anything.

'If she . . .' Shu-chun stopped short before she finally got it out, 'really cares for you, would you like her?'

'What you say is meaningless, how can I answer? I don't even know her name, and I haven't seen her, how can I talk about liking her? Besides, I. . . .'

'You *have* seen her,' Shu-chun interrupted quickly, afraid that he would bring out his 'plans' and then it would be difficult to get back to the subject. 'If she is one you have seen, could you like her?'

'One person can't become fond of another just like that.'

'Then there is already someone in your heart?' she asked anxiously, her heart thumping away.

'No,' Ta-chun answered, quietly and briefly.

'No one at all? Not one in the village whom you like?'

'No.' His reply was still brief, but he seemed to have great difficulty in keeping calm.

'Very well, then, let's go.' She stood up decidedly, pouting.

'What's the hurry? Let's sit a while longer, there's no wind here.' Her decided action made him waver a little.

'It's cold even without any wind, and there's work to do tomorrow. . . .'

'Who hasn't got work to do?'

'It's getting late, the moon's in the west, let's go.' She felt hurt and hung her head.

'If you insist, let's go. What I mean is, since we've got here, we may as well sit a bit longer.'

'What's the sense in just sitting?'

They both got up, came out of the wood-shed, and walked down the hill, one after the other; the moonlight filtering through the trees played on their bodies and faces. Sheng Shu-chun, walking in front, didn't turn her head at all and as her feet felt for the path in the knee-deep spear-grass, she was thinking, it must be her home, her mother's former bad reputation, that made him look down upon her. As she reflected, she felt sorry for herself and wept silently. By now they had got down to a thickly wooded slope. Shu-chun was so absorbed in her thoughts that she carelessly trod on a patch of slippery moss, slid, and fell backwards. Ta-chun caught her in his arms and she turned and fell on his breast. The tears on her pale face sparkling in the moonlight startled him, and he hastily asked:

'What's the matter? Why are you crying all of a sudden?'

'I'm not crying, I'm happy.' She smiled through her tears, looking more lovable then ever. The interplay of emotion and sudden physical contact caused their relationship to undergo a great qualitative change. His male seriousness and her girlish pride gave way completely to an involuntary and fiery abandon, an unconditional yielding to each other. He embraced her with all his strength, holding her waist so tightly against his own body that it hurt and she cried out. He felt something thumping violently inside her soft breast against his broad chest. Her arms embraced his neck and brought her burning face closer to his.

After a while, she looked up, and her hands gently stroked his short, rather coarse hair. She said with a smile, rather as if it were an order from a young girl accustomed to coy behaviour:

'Look at me and tell me honestly, no flattery allowed, do you. . . .' There was a pause and then she bravely asked:

'Do you like me?'

28 SEIZE THE DAY, SEIZE THE HOUR!

Nothing captures the mood of China in the 1960s better than this short, urgent poem by Mao Tse-tung, penned in his bold and sweeping calligraphy. The Great Leap Forward (1958-60) in which the 'People's Communes' were set up had come and gone, shifting Chinese society several degrees further left towards socialism but causing some economic chaos made worse by three years of unusually bad weather. The Soviet Union, withdrawing all its aid and technical assistance at a critical time, had added to China's difficulties. In the winter of 1962 the Soviet premier Nikita Khrushchev began to criticise the Chinese publicly and within six months the Sino-Soviet split would become a subject for bitter polemics on both sides. In Mao's poem, Khrushchev is one of the flies who 'dash themselves against the wall'. He is like the man in a Chinese legend who fell asleep under a locust tree and dreamt that he married the princess of

Seizing the hour. A river is straightened to gain more land

a great kingdom. But when he awoke, he found that the kingdom was just an ants' nest under the tree. At home too there were critics of the Great Leap Forward who argued for less emphasis on class struggle, more moderate economic policies. To them Mao answers that life is too short for caution. Besides, all over the world people are rising to assert their own destiny. There is so much to be done and China has the strength to do it.

Mao Tse-tung—9 January 1963

On this tiny globe
A few flies dash themselves against the wall,
Humming without cease,
Sometimes shrilling,
Sometimes moaning.
Ants on the locust tree assume a great nation swagger
And mayflies lightly plot to topple the giant tree.
The west wind scatters leaves over Changan,
And the arrows are flying, twanging.

So many deeds cry out to be done,
And always urgently;
The world rolls on,
Time presses.
Ten thousand years are too long,
Seize the day, seize the hour!

The Four Seas are rising, clouds and waters raging,
The Five Continents are rocking, wind and thunder roaring.
Away with all pests!
Our force is irresistible.

In 1959 the Chinese Minister of Defence, Peng Teh-huai, critical of the Great Leap Forward and less suspicious than Mao of Soviet intentions, was replaced by Lin Piao. Under Lin the People's Liberation Army began to remould itself into a highly political instrument in some ways more receptive to Mao's teachings than the Communist Party itself. The armed forces set an example for the rest of the nation, showing it how to maintain the old revolutionary traditions of honesty, frugality and hard work after the fighting stage of revolution was over. Lei Feng, a model army hero whose virtues are praised below, was the kind of young man, dedicated to socialism and to 'serving the people', whom China's youth were now urged to emulate. In this way they could become worthy 'revolutionary successors' to the present generation.

'Why Millions Honour Lei Feng', from China Reconstructs, *June 1963*

The name Lei Feng is on the lips of millions of men, women and children in China today. An ordinary soldier who became a squad leader in a transport company of the People's Liberation Army, Lei Feng set an immortal example for others in his life of twenty-two years, cut short by a lorry accident on 15 August last year [1962]. A product of our age, he was typical of the countless heroes who rise from the ranks of the people in the struggle for socialism.

Lei Feng was born in a poor peasant family, and in his childhood he knew all the hunger, poverty, cruelty and degradation of the old society. Only after the liberation was he able to eat regularly and go to school with books under his arm. Before joining the army in 1960, he worked as a tractor driver on a county-run state farm, and then in the Anshan Iron and Steel Company in northeast China. His deeds and the thick notebooks of his diary, totalling some 200,000 words, show his single-minded devotion to the noble ideal of working for the happiness of mankind and his constant concern with the problem of how to speed the building of socialism. Selfless and anxious to help others, he led a simple life and studied perseveringly. Full of youthful vigour, he was diligent and modest. . . .

On 3 December 1959 a report was given in his workshop on the need for conscription, and its aims. Early the next morning Lei Feng signed up at the enlistment station. As he was below the standards for height and weight, he raised his heels a little when being measured and pressed hard on the scales when being weighed. 'I haven't had breakfast yet, otherwise I would reach the minimum,' he explained. While examining him, the doctor saw many deep scars on his body and asked him how he had got them. 'They are the marks of hatred carved on me by the old society,' he answered, 'I want to join the army so that others will never need to bear such scars. Our country is still menaced by imperialists and my heart urges me to take up arms to defend the motherland.' His words moved everyone present. After repeated entreaties, an exception was made for him and he was accepted.

8 January 1960 was Lei Feng's first day in the army. He bought a new diary for the occasion. On the first page he stuck a picture of Huang Chi-kuang, the national hero who lost his life in the Korean war. Lei Feng looked at this picture every day and never ceased trying to measure up to his ideal.

Training of the new recruits began. Given a hand grenade, Lei Feng found that he could not throw it the required distance, however hard he tried. He was very worried. When he was writing in his diary after supper that night, his eyes fell on the picture of Huang Chi-kuang. He picked up the practice grenade, went to the drill ground, stationed himself facing the north wind, and threw it again and again. He was still at it when the squad leader found him long after the Lights Out bugle had sounded. His whole body ached so much after his efforts that he couldn't sleep. But he reminded himself in his diary, 'Think how you were tortured by scabies when you were a boy! Now you are training in order to be able to defend your homeland. Why should a little pain bother you?'

The political instructor in his unit lent him books telling how other people had overcome difficulties. After he had read them, he wrote, 'When the struggle is most severe, victory is close. But this is also the moment when one may falter. It is the critical juncture for everyone. . . . Difficulties harbour the seed of victory and failures are the breeding-ground of success.' He encouraged himself, 'Be a pine tree in the tempest rather than a weak seedling in a greenhouse.' He continued with his rigorous practising. A few weeks later he was able to make a high score in a test of accuracy in hand grenade throwing.

A little later Lei Feng was transferred to be a lorry driver in a

A model soldier serves the people – tea in the fields

transport squad. Elated, he composed the following verse:

> A lad's dream has come true,
> For the first time he wears a uniform;
> As he looks at himself in the mirror
> A golden phoenix rises from his heart!
> Assigned by the Party to drive a lorry,
> Behind the wheel he takes the utmost care.
> He keeps his machine polished bright as a mirror,
> Treasuring it as the apple of his eye.

Lei Feng became so absorbed with his studies that he often sat up until after midnight. He bought a flashlight so that he could read under the quilt when everyone else was asleep. 'After studying Chairman Mao's writings,' he wrote, 'I begin to understand how and for what to live. . . .' As his awareness deepened he set down thoughts such as: 'Two-thirds of the poor in the world are not yet liberated. Oppressed and exploited, they are underfed and lacking in clothes. I cannot look on while they are mistreated.'

Lei Feng held rigidly to a simple life. Except for what he spent for haircuts and the purchase of soap and some books, he banked all of his monthly allowance. He sewed cotton patches on his socks until there was practically nothing of the originals to be seen, and his wash basin and cup were covered with spots where the enamel had chipped off.

But Lei Feng was always ready to give help where help was needed. While he was stationed in Fushun, he saw people beating gongs and drums in the streets to announce the formation of a people's commune. Immediately, he rushed to the bank, withdrew the 200 yuan that he had in his account and took it to the commune office. He wanted to contribute to its reserve fund, he explained. When the commune leaders refused to accept the money and suggested he send it home, he said, 'Home? This is my home. Except for the people I have nothing. The people have given me everything. Let this money play its part for the benefit of the people!' Moved by his earnestness and sincerity, the commune finally accepted half the sum. He took back the hundred *yuan* balance but when he read there was a serious flood round the town of Liaoyang, he sent it to aid the people who had suffered in the disaster.

On one occasion a member of Lei Feng's squad received a letter from his ailing father which surprised him greatly. 'I received your remittance of ten *yuan*,' the father wrote his son. 'My illness has taken a turn for the better. I hope you will concentrate on your job in the army and not worry about me. . . .' It was Lei Feng who, hearing that the sick man was in financial difficulty, had sent him the money in the son's name.

For such actions, and because he refused to spend a penny on himself, some people called Lei Feng 'a fool'. On this he wrote in his diary, 'Those who say I am a fool are wrong. My only desire is to be useful to the people and the country. If that is being a fool, I am glad to be one, for the revolution needs such fools, and so does the construction of our motherland.'

-3 FOUR RED GUARD DOCUMENTS FROM THE CULTURAL REVOLUTION

The Cultural Revolution was more than a political struggle against a few high-level Party Leaders like China's Head of State Liu Shao-chi. It spread throughout society as a mass movement against all forms of thought and behaviour which were not in keeping with Mao's brand of revolutionary socialism. Bureaucracy, self-interest, 'bourgeois behaviour', authoritarianism, 'looking down on the masses', excessive emphasis on material incentives, these and other targets of the Cultural Revolution were personified in Liu Shao-chi and the 'small handful' of Party leaders who, it was claimed, wished to 'restore capitalism' in China, and had dragged their feet during and since the Great Leap Forward. But at the local level the Cultural Revolution got to grips with basic social values and relationships. The first Red Guards were secondary school students in Peking; the whole country's educational system was suspended for three years while the students struggled and argued over how to end 'élitist' attitudes towards education. In Extract 30 students from a Peking girls' school put forward a plan for reforming the college entrance system which was substantially accepted after the Cultural Revolution (see further pp. 203–6).

In industry rebel workers sought (eventually with less success) to abolish material incentives and to gain a bigger say in running their own factories. Early in 1967 some of Mao's opponents in charge of the Party apparatus in Shanghai and other industrial centres tried to blunt the Revolution by buying off the workers. Extract 31 describes how this attempt was denounced by one group of cotton-mill workers as a policy of 'economism'.

As the Cultural Revolution continued into 1967 and 1968 some Red Guard groups with backing from 'ultra-left' leaders in Peking argued for a more thorough revolution than Mao himself thought practicable. Suspicious of all authority, including the People's Liberation Army which had moved in to quell fighting between the rival Red Guard factions and keep the country's economy going, the ultra-leftists came close to advocating anarchism. In Extract 32, a group called the *Sheng-wu-lien* in Hunan province denounces the army as just another form of bureaucracy, and defends those Red Guards who had seized weapons from military units and the militia. In summer 1968 after bloodshed in several provinces Mao authorised the armed forces, supported by local workers and peasants, to move in and pacify (mostly by argument rather than by force) the student Red Guards. Most of the Red Guards were then sent to the countryside to reform themselves through labour; the Party and government administration began slowly to be rebuilt. In Extract 33 the Commander of the Nanking Military Region rebukes students at the Nanking Engineering Institute for fighting among themselves.

30 DOWN WITH THE FEUDAL EXAMS

Letter from Peking No. 1 Girls' Middle School

Dear Central Committee of the Party and dear Chairman Mao, you place boundless hopes on us. You have said: 'The world is as much yours as ours but ultimately it is yours. You young people are full of vitality and at a stage of vigorous growth; you are like the sun at eight or nine in the morning. We put our hopes on you. . . . The world belongs to you and the future of China belongs to you.'

Dear Central Committee of the Party and dear Chairman Mao, we are students who will soon graduate from senior middle school. In this great cultural revolution, the responsibility falls first of all on our shoulders to smash the old college entrance examination system. We wish to express our views on the existing system of admittance to higher schools.

We hold that the existing system of admittance to higher schools is a continuation of the old feudal examination system dating back thousands of years. It is a most backward and reactionary educational system. It runs counter to the educational policy laid down by Chairman Mao. . . . In fact it is extending and prolonging the three major differences – between manual and mental labour, between worker and peasant and between town and country. Concretely, we make the following charges against it:

1.   Many young people are led not to study for the revolution but to immerse themselves in books for the university entrance examination and to pay no heed to politics. Quite a number of students have been indoctrinated with such gravely reactionary ideas of the exploiting classes as that 'book learning stands above all else' of 'achieving fame', 'becoming experts', 'making one's own way', 'taking the road of becoming bourgeois specialists', and so on. The present examination system encourages these ideas.

2.   It makes many schools chase one-sidedly after a high rate in the number of their students who will be admitted to higher schools and as a result many become 'special' and 'major' schools which specially enrol 'outstanding students'. These schools have opened the gates wide to those who completely immerse themselves in books and pay no attention to politics and have shut out large numbers of outstanding children of workers, peasants and revolutionary cadres.

3.   It seriously hampers students from developing morally, intellectually and physically and particularly morally. This system fundamentally ignores the ideological revolutionisation of the youth. It is, in essence, exactly what is preached by the sinister Teng To gang: 'teaching one in accordance with his ability' and 'using one in accordance with his ability'.

Respected and beloved Chairman Mao, you have repeatedly taught us that 'We should support whatever the enemy opposes and oppose whatever the enemy supports'. As the enemy claps his hands and applauds the old system so desperately, can we allow it to continue to exist? No! Not for a single day! Today, in this great and unprecedented cultural revolution, we must join the workers, peasants and soldiers in smashing it thoroughly. We suggest in concrete terms that:

1.   Beginning this year, we abolish the old system of enrolling students to the higher schools.

2.   Graduates from senior middle schools should go straight into

Liu and his wife are feted by President Sukarno on a 'bourgeois' state visit to Indonesia

Liu and courtiers in his 'black palace'

Cartoons from the Red Guard press satirising China's Head of State Liu Shao-chi for his 'capitalist' policies

Liu puts China through the hoop of 'revisionism'

the midst of the workers, peasants and soldiers and integrate themselves with the masses.

We think that at a time when their world outlook is being formed, young people of seventeen or eighteen years old should be tempered and nurtured in the storms of the three great revolutionary movements (of class struggle, the struggle for production and scientific experimentation). They should first of all get 'ideological diplomas' from the working class and the poor and lower middle peasants. The Party will select the best from among the fine sons and daughters of the proletariat, young people who truly serve the broad masses of workers, peasants and soldiers, and send them on to higher schools. We absolutely do not agree that one should go among the workers, peasants and soldiers after one's graduation from college because at that time one's world outlook will have basically been formed, and any remoulding will have become difficult. Moreover, some persons who have acquired 'knowledge' think that they have got the 'capital' to bargain with the Party and the people. . . .

The Chinese revolution as well as the world revolution call on us to be the revolutionary vanguard of the world's youth. We must be those who dare to think, to speak, to do, to break through and to make revolution. We know the road we are going to take is a new road, a new road that leads to communism. We must and can tread out our proletarian road. Of course, we will still meet many 'tigers' on the road of revolution. But can revolutionary youth be frightened by them? We regard the obstacles put up by backward ideologies, by our families, and by public opinion as nothing. We are determined to cleave through and to overpower the ill winds and evil forces! What we need is the dauntless, heroic spirit of a revolutionary who 'knows there are tigers on the mountain, but insists on taking that road'.

Dear Central Committee of the Party, dear Chairman Mao, please rest assured! We are fully prepared to wipe out all the tigers on our way! We have a most extremely powerful weapon – Mao Tse-tung's great thought. With that weapon in our hands we will fear nothing, neither heaven nor earth, nor any monsters.

Wang Kuan-hua in China Reconstructs, *April 1967*

Not long ago the ill wind of economism swept through our Shanghai No. 17 State Cotton Mill. The handful of persons in authority in the Party who were taking the capitalist road suddenly became most 'concerned' about us. They repeatedly asked us proletarian revolutionaries what grievances we had about the welfare arrangements in the mill. The man responsible for labour protection once sought me out and, assuming an air of great concern for my well-being, asked, 'Do you need anything? How about a new jacket and a pair of leather shoes to begin with?' How 'modest' and 'warmhearted' he suddenly appeared!

For years we workers in the machine repair shop had been raising questions of labour protection, but some still remained unsolved. We refrained from bringing it up during the cultural revolution because we wanted to concentrate on the rebellion against the handful of persons in authority within the Party who were taking the capitalist road and the bourgeois reactionary line. Now all of a sudden this rotten handful in authority were pressing the matter. I wondered why. This was really most unusual! Then I recalled Chairman Mao's teaching: 'Communits must always go into the whys and wherefores of anything, use their own heads and carefully think over whether or not it corresponds to reality and is really well founded; on no account should they follow blindly and encourage slavishness.' I began asking myself many questions. Why is this ill wind of economism sweeping through society with such force? Why should it appear now at this critical stage of the battle between the two lines? I also recalled Chairman Mao's teaching: 'Our point of departure is to serve the people whole-heartedly and never for a moment divorce ourselves from the masses, to proceed in all cases from the interests of the people and not from one's self-interest or from the interests of a small group, and to identify our responsibility to the people with our responsibility to the leading organs of the Party.'

Suddenly the whole thing became clear to me. This is definitely not a mere matter of a jacket and a pair of leather shoes. This is a vicious political plot by the handful of persons in authority within

'Down with economism!' A revolutionary poster

the Party who were taking the capitalist road. Under the pretext of 'correcting shortcomings', using economism as the bait, they are trying to corrupt and divide the proletarian revolutionaries, divert a serious political struggle onto the wrong road of economism, and in this way to strangle the proletarian cultural revolution. If they succeed, they would then turn around and strike back at us proletarian revolutionaries and slanderously accuse us of rebelling to further our own private interests. We must not be taken in!

Armed with the thought of Chairman Mao, my answer to the rotten handful was decisive and clear, 'We don't want new jackets or leather shoes. We want Mao Tse-tung's thought and the proletarian revolutionary line represented by Chairman Mao!'

---

32 GRABBING ARMS IS FINE!

From 'Whither China', a manifesto of the Sheng-wu-lien

Any revolution must necessarily involve the army. Since a Red capitalist class has already been formed in China, it follows that the army cannot detach itself from this reality. But the January Revolution [of 1967] has not touched in any way upon the vital problem of all revolutions – the question of the army . . .

1.   It can now be seen that the army of today is different from the people's army of before the Liberation [in 1949]. Before Liberation the army and the people fought together to overthrow imperialism, bureaucratic capitalism and feudalism. Their relationship was like that between fish and water. After Liberation, the revolution shifted from its former targets to hit at the capitalist-roaders. Since the capitalist-roaders hold power in the army, some elements in it have not only discarded their flesh-and-blood relations with the people, but have even become tools for suppressing revolution.

If, therefore, the Great Proletarian Cultural Revolution is to succeed, a radical change in the army is called for. The fact is that in the same year that Chairman Mao issued the order for the armed forces to live in their barracks, they became divorced from the masses.

2.   It can now be seen that we need to have a revolutionary war in the country if the revolutionary people of today in China want

Little Red Guards, from a primary-school, Sian

160

High school students march out to the countryside for a camping exercise

to overthrow the armed Red capitalist class. . . . The local revolutionary wars which were waged in August this year [1967] have given us a rich experience which is unparalleled in history. . . . Large-scale gun-seizing incidents [by the Red Guards] took place regularly. . . . Local wars of various sizes, in which the army was sometimes directly involved, erupted in the country. . . . For a short time the cities were in a state of 'armed mass dictatorship'. . . . The heroic image of the primary-school pupils who volunteered to work as traffic police, and the pride with which some mass organisations ran financial and economic affairs, has left an unforgettable impression. . . .

The arms-grabbing movement of August 1967 was great! It was not only unprecedented in the capitalist world, but it also managed to turn the whole nation into soldiers for the first time in any socialist country. Before the Cultural Revolution the bureaucrats were scared to hand over arms to the people – the Militia was only a façade behind which they controlled the armed strength of the people. But now the masses, instead of receiving arms like favours from above, for the first time seized from the bureaucrats by their own brute force. For the first time the workers had their 'own' arms.

But the proclamation of the September 5 Directive [ordering the rebels to return their weapons] completely nullified Chairman Mao's rousing call to 'arm the Left'. The working class was disarmed. The bureaucrats again came back to power.

33 WHY MUST WE FIGHT?

From a speech by the Commander of Nanking Military Region

The purpose of my coming here is to see you comrades. I hope that you students of the Nanking Engineering Institute will listen to Chairman Mao and follow his instruction. We mustn't have the kind of situation where one faction suppresses another and arrests the other's people. We must have harmony among ourselves and hatred against the enemy. . . .

You must constantly remind yourselves that we are all revolutionary comrades. Why should we fight one another? Why should we quarrel with one another? Why should we be angry with one

Back in class after the Cultural Revolution, students in a Peking school workshop assemble components for cars. Productive labour is an important part of the new education

another? Aren't there some military works [of yours] that haven't been dismantled? Why must we fight? If you want to fight, I can take you to Vietnam to fight the enemy.

In learning engineering, you have to learn from us workers and soldiers. As for the study of machine-building, we also have something to offer you. We have many types of machinery. This applies to architecture too. We are stronger than you. As for bridges – you can only draw, but you know nothing about the actual operation. . . .

It is necessary to seize power from the hands of the old intellectuals, so that their domination of our schools will be ended for good. Now many of you students are wearing glasses. On one occasion I could see for myself that one-third of the students of Nanking University were wearing glasses. If you don't solve the problem of the old intellectuals, many more of you will have to wear glasses. You would all be trying desperately to get your 'ten out of ten'. I am in my sixties now, but my eyesight is still very good. When I go out hunting, I can still see clearly a moving wild duck several hundred metres away. And I never made any effort to get 'ten out of ten'. . . .

Nanking University has sent its students to cut wheat in the suburbs, but you haven't been asked to. When autumn comes, you will be asked to go and cut beans. If we depended on the students of your two colleges alone to cut wheat, you would never finish the job before your beards turned grey. Luckily we depend chiefly on machines. . . .

You must set up Revolutionary Committees quickly, and when they have been set up, our troops will be withdrawn. (The audience: Please don't take them away!) They cannot be withdrawn at present, of course, because you are still fighting one another.

---

34 EVERYDAY LIFE AFTER THE CULTURAL REVOLUTION

One of the most conspicuous results of the Cultural Revolution has been the way in which local communities have acquired more responsibility for running their own affairs. In the new Revolutionary

Committees, established in factories, communes, schools and all other administrative units, local representatives share authority with government and Communist Party officials. Most schools and hospitals are now run and financed by the communities which they serve. In the countryside many more small factories have been set up under the control of the county or people's commune, making farm machinery, fertiliser, cement and bricks, and other basic industrial products on the spot where they are needed.

Almost everyone is involved in some way or other with what goes on in his own neighbourhood. The Chinese people have the same concerns as people elsewhere – with their families, food, housing and schools. But they solve their problems collectively; the distinction between private and public is less sharp than in most other societies. In the following interview, recorded by a foreign resident in Peking in March 1972, the woman Chairman of the Revolutionary Committee of a 'Street Committee' describes how they run the affairs of the Feng Shen neighbourhood. (The Street Committee manages not one but two main streets, plus 120 *hu-tung* or lanes running off them, with a total population of over 50,000.) She starts with the Committee's organisational structure, and then goes on to discuss health, housing, schools and crime.

Hsu Chung-chi, Chairman of Feng Shen Revolutionary Committee

The main responsibility of our Street Committee is to mobilise the masses in the area under the unified leadership of the party in the three great revolutions, of class-struggle, production and scientific experiment. We organise our people for political, economic and industrial work, and for cultural and health work; we also look after social security. We are responsible, too, for the masses' daily affairs – environmental hygiene, registration of marriages, conciliation of petty disputes and frictions, divorces or reconciliation, and the re-education of minor delinquents and revisionists. In carrying out all these functions, we mainly rely on the broad masses and mass organisations. Under our Street Committee, there are twenty-five Inhabitants' Sub-Committees. Each sub-committee is responsible for three to five lanes. The members of these committees are elected by the masses, and they work on a voluntary basis for self-government. There are also group leaders in each lane. Beside security affairs, health propaganda, the cleaning of the lanes, traffic control, etc., these sub-committees and groups organise political study-

A covered market in a Shanghai housing estate. The slogan is in support of a public health campaign

Early morning rush-hour in Peking. The bicycle rules the road

Two generations in a Shanghai housing estate

classes and newspaper study groups. This is how the masses raise their ideological consciousness and take part in state affairs. . . .

We run a hospital too. It was set up in 1960 by merging some privately owned clinics of pre-liberation days. Yes, by 1956 these clinics had already been taken over by the State. The hospital is a collective and is mainly run on its own income. Initially, the Managing Office of the Street Committee gave some help, while the District Public Health Bureau gave us the personnel. There are now eighty-two doctors and staff members. They draw fixed salaries from the hospital's own funds. The fees that the patients have to pay are ten cents for diagnosis and, of course, the price of any medicine prescribed. But, as you know, recently prices of medicine have been drastically reduced. Take the case of a phial of penicillin. The price has been reduced from one *yuan* to twenty cents per phial. Cost of a Tetracyclene tablet is only five cents. Besides, in various enterprises and factories, we also have clinics where workers themselves get free medical facilities and their family-members have to pay only half the normal fees. In the hospital we combine both western and traditional treatment. We have one specialised group for propaganda work in public health and hygiene and one for planned parenthood. The group for family planning works under the general guidance of the Health and Cultural Group of the Revolutionary Committee and operates through mass organisations, like the Inhabitants' Sub-Committees, and the twenty-five stations. Contraceptive pills are supplied free. In this field we have achieved some success. Take the case of the area under the Ta Cheng Sub-Committee. There are around 400 households; fifty-six women of child-bearing age in that area have not given birth during the last three years. We do not disturb the young couples. We do our propaganda work mainly with those having more than three children. The young people now are all working. So they themselves are conscious of the problem of having too many children in quick succession.

As we told you before, there are twenty-five health stations. These were mostly set up after the Cultural Revolution, in 1970. The masses established them on their own initiative. Beside preventive work and simple treatments, health workers in these stations mainly practise traditional methods – acupuncture, massage, herbal medicines. . . .

With regard to housing, we have so far succeeded in providing shelter for every family in our area. There is a housing office under the Revolutionary Committee which looks after the maintenance of all houses, including repair facilities like electricity, running water, etc. This office also prepares its own plan for the utilisation of existing houses and arranges for exchange of houses. For example, we try to provide houses for people that are near their places of work. Of course, we work in close co-ordination with the District Housing Bureau. As for building new houses, this is done under the unified plan of the Municipal Revolutionary Committee.

The rental of a house is very low, only twenty-five cents per square metre. For running water, the fee is four cents per member of the family. The cost of electricity comes to around one *yuan* a month for a household. However, heating facilities must be arranged by the people themselves. Normally they buy their own stove and also a pipe for letting out the smoke. They use the stove for both cooking and heating. Besides, as you know, every worker gets around sixteen *yuan* each winter as a heating allowance from the enterprise for which he or she is working. Normally in a household, there are at least two members who are working. The allowance they get is sufficient to cover the running costs, and part of the initial cost, of a stove. Most of the houses are old. There are four houses around a square courtyard. Normally, one water tap is shared by the families living around the courtyard. Yes, the privies are also shared.

Before a young couple registers their marriage, we manage to provide them with a room, if they want it. It is up to the couple to decide where the wedding ceremony is to take place. Normally, they choose a place near their new house.

Yes, all the houses are State-owned. As you know, we confiscated the houses of bureaucrat-capitalists immediately after liberation. We allowed the national capitalists to retain their houses. But many of them voluntarily surrendered. By 1956, when we had achieved the stage of joint State-private enterprises, all houses became State-owned. Still, some of the old capitalists continued to use part of their old houses for themselves. We had one such case in Ta Cheng neighbourhood. Shi Chang-chou, an old landlord, retained the middle-courtyard houses for himself. During the Cultural Revolution, the Red Guards swept him out of them and sent him back to his home village in the north-east to receive re-education from the poor peasants.

Since the Cultural Revolution we have also taken over the responsibility of running the primary schools. Previously, these schools were under the District Educational Bureau. There are ten such schools in our area with 460 teachers and staff members.

The salaries of the teachers are paid by the State. Other expenditures are met from school fees and Street Committee grants. The student fee is nominal – two to three *yuan* per term, four to six *yuan* a year.

We also run four kindergartens, three of which have nurseries attached. They handle more than six hundred children. The age range of the children stretches from fifty-six days old to six years old. We set up the kindergartens in 1955 to help working parents. Yes, they were organised by housewives on a voluntary basis. A small fee was charged from the parents for feeding the children. Now of course it is different. The teachers in the kindergartens and the caretakers of the nurseries get a fixed salary. Take the case of the kindergarten in Ta Cheng neighbourhood. It was started in 1955 by eight housewives and was enlarged in 1958. Now there are forty-three teachers and staff members. There are 141 children in the kindergarten aged three to seven, while there are sixty-two children in the nursery. In the kindergarten there are five classes and three grades. The teachers are housewives and young middle-school graduates. The average salary of a teacher is thirty *yuan*. The young school graduates get an allowance of sixteen *yuan* a month for the first one or two years. Of course, they get other facilities like free medical care, transport, working clothes, etc.

There are two systems in these kindergartens and nurseries, one is day-care and one is day-and-night care. For day-care with three meals and fruit after the midday nap, parents have to pay around twelve *yuan* a month; for day-and-night care, sixteen *yuan* a month. Normally the women workers in State District or Street enterprises get half that amount in allowance from their factories and workshops.

We also run a General Service Station. It offers various kinds of services like repairs to household utensils, mending of clothes and shoes, sewing and tailoring, etc. There are also smaller outlets in various neighbourhoods which offer subsidiary services to the inhabitants. . . .

There are, of course, still cases of petty pilferage and other minor crimes. But major crimes like stealing, robbery or murder have not taken place in the last three years. So long as classes exist there will be crimes. But the main feature of our security work is to depend on the masses, rather than on power organs, for re-educating delinquents. In minor cases, like pilferage or street-fighting, normally the organisations concerned, to which the delinquents belong, organise mass meetings to criticise and re-educate the offenders. The neighbourhood groups very often take care of small disputes and con-

Tuning up. Amateur musicians in the pavilion of a public park

Bicycle porters waiting for work in a Canton street.

troversies. Cases involving young students we refer to the parents or the school. Sometimes the security group of the Street Committee also mobilises the masses for re-education in such cases.

For the serious crimes, however, the power organs of the Proletarian Dictatorship take charge. There are the People's courts at the District level and the public security office of the State. The Street Committee, of course, supports the People's court in ferreting out criminals and hidden counter-revolutionaries. The Committee also organises mass-criticism meetings to expose such criminals. But it is only the People's court which has the authority to convict them or impose sentences in individual cases.

But, as I just told you, due to the heightening of proletarian consciousness the security situation is steadily improving. In many families everyone goes out to work. Sometimes they do not even lock the door. Yet they are not worried. They know that the neighbours will look after their houses. The house is the rear area. To guarantee its safety is to guarantee victory in the front-line struggle for production.

Since the Cultural Revolution the Street Committee also looks after divorce cases. Previously, people had to file petitions for divorce to the District Courts. This system has been discarded, and now it is as it should be. We know the inhabitants of our area better and more intimately. In our country, the question of divorce is a very serious one. If people are encouraged to divorce freely, it will involve a question of social morality. . . .

Finally, a word about living conditions. You may say that our workers do not earn a very high salary. But they are guaranteed a reasonable life. In this area the cost of food for one person averages around ten *yuan* a month. We have made some investigations in one inhabitants' group of 150 households. Before liberation they had among them only one bicycle and seven pocket-watches and all these were owned by bureaucrats and capitalists. Now there are 189 wrist-watches, 152 bicycles, 160 transistor radios and 45 sewing-machines. In Chinese we say that our aim is to let every household have 'Three Wheels (a bicycle, a sewing-machine and a wrist-watch) and One Carry (a transistor radio)'.

FACTS,
FIGURES
AND
FURTHER
READING

At the end of each section I have suggested some titles for further reading, as far as possible choosing works which are either in paperback or likely to be found on library shelves. A good start could be made with the three-volume collection of readings, *Imperial China – Republican China – Communist China,* edited by Franz Schurmann and Orville Schell (Penguin Books, 1968). English-language books published in Peking are mostly out of print, but some are being reissued.

China today

U. S. S. R.

MONGOLIA

Ulan Bator

SINKIANG

INNER MONGOLIA

HEILUNGKIANG

Harbin

Kirin

KIRIN

Mukden

LIAONING

Peking

HOPEH

Taiyuan

Tientsin

TSINGHAI

Sining

NINGHSIA

SHANSI

Tsinan

SHANTUNG

Tsingtao

Lanchow

KANSU

Sian

SHENSI

HONAN

KIANGSU

Nanking

Shanghai

TIBET

Lhasa

SZECHWAN

Chengtu

HUPEH

Wuhan

ANHWEI

CHEKIANG

Chungking

Changsha

Nanchang

KIANGSI

Foochow

KWEICHOW

HUNAN

FUKIEN

Kunming

Kweiyang

Amoy

YUNNAN

Liuchow

KWANGSI

KWANGTUNG

Canton

TAIWAN

HAINAN

National Autonomous Regions

174

IMPERIAL CHINA

DYNASTIES

HSIA	*c.* 21st-16th century BC	*Pre-history*
SHANG	*c.* 16th-11th century BC	
CHOU	*c.* 11th century-221 BC	*Recorded history*
Spring and Autumn Period	770-475 BC	
Warring States Period	475-221 BC	
CHIN	221-206 BC	*First unified state*
HAN	206 BC-AD 220	
Former (or Western) Han	206 BC-AD 24	
Later (or Eastern) Han	25-220	
THREE KINGDOMS	220-280	
TSIN	265-420	
SOUTHERN AND NORTHERN DYNASTIES	420-589	
SUI	589–618	
TANG	618-907	
FIVE DYNASTIES	907-960	
SUNG	960-1279	
Northern Sung	960-1127	
Southern Sung	1127-1279	
YUAN (Mongol)	1279-1368	
MING	1368-1644	
CHING (Manchu)	1644-1911	

The Emperor's rule extended to the 'four corners of the earth'; he enjoyed, so it was said, the Mandate of Heaven – at least until he was overthrown by war, rebellion or palace intrigue. Other members of the imperial family manoeuvred around the throne, trying to fix the succession to their own advantage. Youthful emperors were particularly vulnerable to the plots of uncles and the influence of eunuchs and concubines.

The scholar-bureaucrats wrote the official histories, kept the records and ran the administration. The examination system, their ladder to promotion, became more complex in the Tang and Sung dynasties, helping to strengthen the bureaucratic machine. Later, during the Ming and Ching dynasties, the imperial court moved to concentrate more authority in its own hands, reducing their power. Confucianism was a very appropriate state ideology which the scholar-bureaucrats vigorously defended in their own interests. For it stressed the importance of authority and obedience, as much in the relationship between government and subjects as between father and son, and it provided the classical texts around which the examination system was constructed. But its arid doctrines had little appeal for the masses, who clung to ancient folk religions and magic cults. Taoism, with its doctrine of *wu-wei* or non-action, and Buddhism, with its emphasis on personal morality and individual equality, also provided popular alternatives to the Confucian orthodoxy from the 4th century AD onwards. (A few emperors were converted to Buddhism, others persecuted it.)

Local officials, landowners and gentry all belonged essentially to the same educated class from which a small minority of scholar-bureaucrats rose to serve the emperor. It was an élite which shared the same economic and political interests, bound together by Confucian culture and by clan ties. From the point of view of the ordinary peasant, the magistrates and the moneylenders, the landlords and the schoolteachers could all be identified as part of the same informal but very effective power-system which kept him in his place.

The emperor and his court, the scholar-gentry network, and the peasants formed the three corners of the triangle – an inverted one with the peasants underneath – which made up the imperial system. (The position of the peasants is discussed in the next section on *Rebellions*.) There were of course vast variations and changes over two thousand years of history, and occasional attempts were made to put right the evils of the system (see Extract 5). Merchants, though scorned in theory, gained more influence from the Sung dynasty onwards as commercial enterprises developed. Soldiers also had much more power in times of unrest than their lowly status in the Confucian hierarchy would suggest.

The impression given in the table above of a unified China throughout the imperial period is also misleading. From the end of the Han to the beginning of the Sui dynasty (AD 220–589) China was divided between north and south, usually with several rival dynasties in each. Those in the north were often founded by nomadic tribes who had become partly 'sinified' – influenced by Chinese culture. After a century of internal division and peasant rebellion the Tang dynasty was succeeded by fifty years of disorder (the Five Dynasties, see

Extract 2). The whole of the second half of the Sung dynasty was confined to south of the Yangtze. In the north the Kin Tartars were succeeded by the Mongols who later established the Yuan dynasty. This was followed by a Chinese restoration (the Ming), succeeded in turn by another foreign house, the Manchus (Ching). China was divided for roughly one-third of its two-thousand-year imperial span; foreign dynasties ruled part or whole of the empire for the same length of time, although they still relied largely on the services of the scholar-bureaucrats for administration.

The Chinese imperial system is described in various ways by Western scholars. It has been called 'oriental despotism', or 'benevolent monarchism', or an 'agrarian-bureaucratic society'. The term 'feudal' is limited to the early Chou period when feudal kingdoms owed allegiance (in theory) to the Chou emperor, before the first real unification in 221 BC and the growth of a central bureaucratic system. Contemporary Chinese writers have fitted their history into a more or less Marxist perspective giving a rather sharper picture, and they use the term 'feudal' for the whole imperial period. They attach particular importance to the peasant rebellions which often speeded the decline of a dynasty, and generally pay more attention than Western writers to the instruments of economic and social change in China's past.

Further reading
A useful quick survey is Tung Chi-ming, *A Short History of China from Earliest Times to 1840* (Peking: Foreign Languages Press (FLP), 1965). The Chinese magazine *China Reconstructs* has often carried articles on imperial and modern history, and the summary below of 'The historical development of Chinese society' is taken from its pages. The various definitions of the Chinese imperial system are usefully discussed by Joseph Levenson & Franz Schurmann, *China: An Interpretative History* (Berkeley: University of California Press, 1969). A slightly old-fashioned but very readable general history is C.P. Fitzgerald's *China: A Short Cultural History* (London: Cresset Press, revised 1961, paperback). W. Eberhard, *A History of China* (London: Routledge and Kegan Paul, 1960) looks more closely at social changes and economic developments. Mark Elvin's *The Pattern of the Chinese Past* (London: Eyre-Methuen, 1973) does so more successfully and should be at the top of any reading list. A more analytical approach, which provides a broad historical perspective, is taken by Michael Loewe, *Imperial China, The Historical Background to the*

Modern Age (London: Allen & Unwin, 1966). None of these books makes very easy reading, but then neither do the classical source materials of Chinese history itself.

THE HISTORICAL DEVELOPMENT OF CHINESE SOCIETY

A Chinese Interpretation from China Reconstructs

Primitive Society: The earliest known tool-making human being living in a primitive society in China was the Peking Man (*Sinanthropus pekinensis*), dating back 500,000 years. Matriarchal clan communities evolved about 50,000 years ago, and agriculture gradually became the main source of livelihood. Patriarchal clan communities emerged approximately 5000 years ago, leading to the formation of tribes and tribal alliances.

Slave Society: During the Hsia dynasty approximately 4000 years back, China entered the stage of slave society and a state ruled by slave-owners was established in the lower reaches of the Yellow River, which became the cradle of ancient Chinese civilisation. The Shang dynasty (seventeenth to eleventh centuries BC) saw the discovery of bronze and the practice of sericulture.

Feudal Society: In the Warring States period (475–221 BC), as the forces of production greatly developed with the wide use of iron tools, slave society was gradually transformed into feudal society.

In 221 BC, Shih Huangti of the Chin dynasty, the builder of the Great Wall, consolidated the first feudal empire in Chinese history, centralising power in the person of an autocratic ruler.

The feudal system lasted more than 2000 years, during which a rich culture was created. The peasant economy was under the control of the emperor, the nobility and the landlords. Exploitation and oppression of the peasants were intense; uprisings and insurrections were unending and frequently on a massive scale.

Semi-Colonial and Semi-Feudal Society: Due to the penetration of foreign imperialism, national capitalism in China never had the opportunity to grow as it did in western countries. As a result of the Opium War which Britain forced on China in 1840 and repeated imperialist aggressions by many countries including Britain, the United States, France, Germany and Japan, the country became semi-colonial and semi-feudal. Imperialists had grasped control of China's vital economic and financial arteries, and its political and military power as well.

The Chinese people suffered greatly under the imperialists and their lackeys. The 1911 Revolution led by the Chinese bourgeoisie destroyed the 2000-year-old absolute monarchy. But the bourgeoisie proved to be incapable of leading the people in overthrowing imperialism and feudalism. It was only after the Chinese Communist Party – vanguard of the working class – assumed the leadership that victory over these enemies became possible.

Socialist Society: The founding of the People's Republic of China in 1949 marked the victory of the new democratic revolution and ushered in the socialist revolution. Socialist society has been established. The country is under the leadership of the working class and based on the worker-peasant alliance. There is democracy for the people (the working class, the peasantry, the urban petty bourgeoisie and the national bourgeoisie), who enforce dictatorship over the landlord class, the bureaucratic-bourgeoisie and the representatives of these classes, and the Kuomintang reactionaries and their accomplices. The Chinese people are now working hard to build up their socialist country.

China Reconstructs (Peking, September 1963)

REBELLIONS

Debt, taxation, forced labour and famine were the main causes of peasant uprisings in imperial China. They were sometimes led by dissident scholars, often were closely connected with secret societies. There was a great variety of motives and goals, but many of these risings expressed a fundamental egalitarian impulse which challenged the privileges of the dominating scholar-gentry class and called for equal distribution of land or other vital economic reforms. Some rebellions were launched in the name of restoring the previous dynasty, although this was probably more of a rallying cry than a practical programme. Religion of some sort, usually connected with Buddhism or Taoism rather than the orthodox Confucianism, was often a source of inspiration. A few uprisings did lead to reforms being made in the countryside, although these were short-lived. They also often precipitated the collapse of a dynasty and were taken advantage of by the incoming dynasty (including the foreign Manchus) to seize power.

The Chinese peasant was not always making rebellion, and his economic position was better at some times than at others. Reforms, often initiated by a new dynasty anxious to make a good start, might lead to an increase in the number of smallholders owning their own land and a decline in the number of tenants and labourers. But in the long run the tendency was always to drift towards landlessness, debt and oppression. Over one thousand peasant uprisings, large or small, have been identified in Chinese history (many others may not have been recorded in the official annals), although scholars outside China have paid comparatively little attention to them. Here is a short list of the largest and best-known:

209-206 BC   The peasant uprising of Chen Sheng and Wu Kuang drastically weakens the Chin dynasty enabling Liu Pang to continue the struggle and found the Han dynasty. Chen and Wu had been sentenced to death for failing to start their military service on time. They raise the revolt with the question 'Are princes, lords, generals and prime ministers a race apart?' Liu Pang repeals the harsh laws of the Chin government.

AD 18-25   The Green Woodsmen and the Red Eyebrows. Thousands of landless peasants rout the armies of the usurping emperor Wang Mang, but in turn are defeated by the first emperor of the Eastern Han dynasty.

184   The Yellow Turbans, whose leader founded a Taoist sect called the Doctrine of Peace, raise a million followers and hold out for twenty years. The Eastern Han dynasty collapses soon after.

875-84   Huang Chao, a salt merchant, leads a rising in south China which spreads north, captures the capital and wages guerrilla war, hastening the decline of the Tang dynasty.

993   Rising led by Wang Hsiao-po, a tea merchant. 'I hate the inequality between poor and rich. Let us level it out.'

1120   Fang La's rising accelerates collapse of Northern Sung dynasty, already under pressure from invading Tartars. The 'Heroes of the Marshes' (Extract 6) are also active.

1351   The Red Turbans rise against the Mongol (Yuan) dynasty. They are defeated but five years later a new Chinese (Ming) dynasty replaces the Mongols.

1630-44   Li Tzu-cheng's peasant army shatters the authority of the

Ming dynasty, captures Peking, is then defeated by the invading Manchus. Resistance in south China continues for twenty years.

1780   Rising of the Hui minority in north-west China.

1795   Rising of the Miao minority in Kweichow and Hunan provinces.

1825-28   Muslim rising in Chinese Turkestan – only partly suppressed at great cost. More Muslim risings there and in Yunnan province, 1860–77.

1850-64   Taiping rebellion spreads from lower Yangtze valley, involves twelve provinces, ruins 600 cities and takes twenty million lives. Inspired by a Christian convert who declares he is the younger brother of Christ. Taiping ideology was a mixture of Christianity, anti-Manchuism, economic egalitarianism.

1853-68   Nien rebellion in eastern China, two million deaths.

1898-1900   The Boxer rebellion (see Extract 14) after famine, floods and foreign penetration in the Yellow River provinces. In 1900 the Boxers besiege the foreign legations in Peking, provoking Western punishment. Other secret societies also active.

Further reading
Unfortunately this is another specialised subject. Jean Chesneaux, *Chinese Secret Societies in the 19th and 20th Centuries* (London: Heinemann, 1961) has documents and commentary. Victor Purcell, *The Boxer Uprising* (Cambridge: Cambridge University Press, 1963) is the best scholarly account with a good feel for the economic background. Accounts of the Western invasion of 1900, e.g. Peter Fleming, *The Siege of Peking* (London: Rupert Hart-Davis, 1959) make good reading but usually fail to do justice to the Chinese view.

EMPIRE

The limits of the Chinese empire fluctuated widely according to the strength of each dynasty and the pressures which it faced from beyond its frontiers. The main threat almost always came from the north, and as early as the first century BC the Great Wall of China was constructed to keep out the 'barbarians'. The stronger dynasties, particularly the Han, Tang and Ching, went beyond the Wall to protect their trade routes to Central Asia and to police the geographical no-man's-land of steppe, mountains and desert against the nomad tribes. Lands to the south and east of China, although some were culturally much closer (e.g. Korea and Vietnam), were untouched by the great nomadic expansions and presented less of a threat. Most formally recognised Chinese 'suzerainty', seeking approval on such occasions as the accession of a new king, and paying regular 'tribute'. Sometimes the payment of tribute indicated a real degree of political dependence upon China, but in other cases tribute was little more than a polite name for trade. In the late eighteenth century, at a time of vigorous expansion under the Manchus, the Chinese empire reached the extent shown below:

North – The Frontier Zones: Mongolia, including both Inner Mongolia (now an Autonomous Region of China) and Outer Mongolia, which was conquered in the eighteenth century but came under Russian influence after 1911, and is now the People's Republic of Mongolia.

Chinese Turkestan, including what is now the Autonomous Region of Sinkiang, on the traditional 'silk route' to Central Asia, previously dominated by China in the Han and Tang dynasties. Colonised and made into a province in the nineteenth century, but a large portion lost to Russia (see p. 186).

Tibet: Mostly independent in early history, the Tibetans even invaded and captured the Chinese capital of Changan in AD 763. But Chinese influence was asserted in the sixteenth century, intervention and sovereignty established in the eighteenth, with Chinese Governors and garrisons stationed in Lhasa. After 1911 control was greatly weakened under British and Russian pressure until the reoccupation of Tibet by the People's Liberation Army in 1950.

South and East – The Tributary States: the following countries paid tribute to China in the nineteenth century until they were detached by the encroaching Western powers (see p. 186): Korea, Ryuku Islands, Annam, Laos, Siam, Burma, Nepal, Sikkim, Bhutan.

Further reading
There has been much discussion, still relevant today, of China's view of the world around her. How far did the Chinese accept in practice the official myth that the whole world owed allegiance to the 'Middle Kingdom' (the literal meaning of the Chinese word for China, *Chung-kuo*)? Did they distinguish in their attitude between different groups of neighbouring countries? Most scholars now agree that although the myth of Chinese supremacy was always

important, China often had a realistic view of the need for state relations with other countries. C.P. Fitzgerald's *The Chinese View of their Place in the World* (London: Oxford University Press, 1964) gives a readable introduction. A volume of essays edited by J.K. Fairbank, *The Chinese World Order* (Cambridge: Harvard University Press, 1968) contains some specialised but important case studies of how imperial diplomacy actually worked.

INVENTIONS

China's economic and technological weakness in the last century was the material basis on which the industrialised West built its dominance. Chinese officials in the nineteenth century, Chinese nationalists in the twentieth, all argued the need to learn Western techniques in order to preserve the essence of China from Western aggression. But until the Industrial Revolution in Europe, Chinese science and technology had been consistently ahead of the West. This subject has been quarried almost single-handed by Dr Joseph Needham at Cambridge University in a series of volumes, still unfinished, on *Science and Civilisation in China*. The first volume (Cambridge, 1961) which gives a general introduction to this field should be in the reference section of every library. Later volumes deal with astronomy, mathematics, geography and cartology, physics and engineering, nautical, military and textile technology, chemistry, biology, agriculture and medicine. Needham gives a brief account of his work in *Hand and Brain in China* (London: Anglo-Chinese Educational Institute, 1971, 20p). Here, from the first volume, is a partial list of Chinese techniques which reached Europe and other regions at times varying between the first and eighteenth centuries AD, and whose use in China antedates those in any other part of the world:

(a) the square-pallet chain-pump (see Extract 7)
(b) the edge-runner mill and the application of power to it
(c) metallurgical blowing-engines operated by water-power
(d) the rotary fan and winnowing machine
(e) the piston-bellows
(f) the horizontal-warp loom (possibly also Indian) and the draw-loom
(g) silk reeling, twisting and doubling machinery
(h) the wheelbarrow
(i) the sailing-carriage

(j) the wagon-mill
(k) the two efficient harnesses for draught animals
(l) the cross-bow
(m) the kite
(n) the helicopter top and the zoetrope
(o) the technique of deep drilling
(p) the mastery of cast iron
(q) the 'Cardan' suspension
(r) the segmental arch bridge
(s) the iron-chain suspension bridge
(t) canal lock-gates
(u) numerous inventions in nautical construction, including water-tight compartments, aerodynamically efficient sails, the fore-and-aft rig
(v) the stern-post rudder
(w) gunpowder and some of its associated techniques
(x) the magnetic compass
(y) paper, printing and movable-type printing
(z) porcelain.

Needham comes to a stop at this point (pp. 240-1) but only because he has exhausted the alphabet. The question still has to be asked why Chinese technological progress never led to an Industrial Revolution or (to put it another way) why capitalism never developed in China. Needham and Mark Elvin (cited under *Dynasties*) both provide some fascinating answers.

LITERATURE

The immense resources of Chinese classical literature defy description in a few words. Here are some of the highlights, mostly available in paperback translations.

Philosophy: The standard translations of Confucius, Mencius and the other Chinese classics by the nineteenth-century missionary-scholar James Legge are still available in reprints but not very readable. Mencius is well served by D.C. Lau's *Mencius* (Penguin Books, 1970), the source of Extract 3. The same author's *Lao Tzu-Tao Te Ching* (Penguin Books, 1963) gives a fine poetic version of this Taoist classic. Arthur Waley has translated the *Analects of Confucius* (Allen & Unwin, 1960).

Poetry and Plays: Arthur Waley's translations of Chinese poetry

184

are poems in their own right, though some prefer more literal translations. A different version of Extract 1 can be found in his *Book of Songs* (Allen & Unwin, 1954). Of his various selections of poems, the most recent edition is *170 Chinese Poems* (Jonathan Cape, 1969). John Scott's *Love and Protest* (Rapp and Whiting, 1972) is less formal and probably easier to read.

Cyril Birch, *Anthology of Chinese Literature* (Penguin Books, 1967) has a large selection of poems up to the fourteenth century and includes prose, plays, and his own translation of Extract 6. Six plays from the Yuan dynasty, early ancestors of what is known as 'Peking opera', are translated by Liu Jung-en in *Six Yuan Plays* (Penguin Books, 1972).

Fiction: The lively market-place tales of the Sung story-tellers were first published in various collections in the Ming dynasty. Cyril Birch, in *Stories from a Ming Collection* (London: Bodley Head, 1958) has translated six of them. A larger selection by Yang Hsien-yi and Gladys Yang is made in *The Courtesan's Jewel Box* (Peking: Foreign Languages Press, 1957).

The great popular novels of the Ming and Ching dynasties are not easy to find in translation; those that exist are mostly incomplete. But look in libraries and anthologies for translations or extracts from the following:

Romance of the Three Kingdoms (Ming) by Lo Kuan-chung, tales of intrigue and warfare in the confused period after the Han dynasty.
Heroes of the Marshes or *Water Margin* (Ming) by Shih Nai-an (Pearl Buck's pre-war translation *All Men Are Brothers* is an abridged version of this novel).
Pilgrimage to the West (Ming) by Wu Cheng-en (abridged by Arthur Waley in *Monkey* (Allen & Unwin).
The Scholars (Ching) by Wu Ching-tzu, a realistic novel of satire on the life of the scholar-gentry (out-of-print Peking translation, Foreign Languages Press, 1957).
Dream of the Red Chamber (Ching) by Tsao Hsueh-chin, *the* great novel of allegory and manners depicting the decline of a wealthy household, which has inspired a whole school of Chinese scholarship – the so-called 'Red'-experts – up to the present day.

All these novels are discussed in *A Brief History of Chinese Fiction* by Lu Hsun (author of Extract 19) (Peking, 1959).

MODERN CHINA

1. Forcing the Door

The Opium War, 1839-41. Treaties of Nanking (British), Wanghsia (US), Whampoa (France), and other agreements. (See Extracts 9 and 10.) Hongkong is ceded, an indemnity to be paid of 21 million silver dollars to cover not only the cost of the British 'expedition' but that of the opium confiscated from British merchants. Five 'Treaty Ports' opened to trade. Two key provisions conceded by the Chinese without understanding their implications for the future: (a) The 'most-favoured-nation' clause, which means that any privilege granted by China to one Western country will be enjoyed by the others; (b) Extra-territoriality. British citizens (hence all other foreigners) in the Treaty Ports to be judged by British, not Chinese, law.

The Second War, 1858-60. Treaties of Tientsin and Peking (Britain, US, France, Russia). (See Extract 11.) The West gains diplomatic access to Peking, twelve new Treaty Ports, the Yangtze opened to foreign navigation, foreigners may travel in the interior, missionaries to be tolerated anywhere in China, import tariffs fixed at five per cent, more indemnities.

2. Peeling the Onion

The West strips off the outer layer of the Chinese sphere of influence, extending its presence to China's borders. This stage culminates in the Boxer Rebellion (see Extract 14), partly a reaction to the spread of foreign control. China must pay indemnity of £67 million.

North-east: One million square kilometres ceded in 1860 to Russia (now part of Soviet Far East).

North-west: Half a million square kilometres of Chinese Turkestan ceded in 1881 to Russia.

Formosa and Ryuku Islands. Occupied by Japan, 1881.

Annam: French suzerainty acknowledged by China, 1885.

Burma: British administration accepted by China, 1886.

Sikkim: Becomes British protectorate, 1890.

Korea: After defeat of Chinese fleet in Sino-Japanese War, Korea becomes 'independent' under Japanese influence, 1895.

China 1911

MANCHURIA

OUTER MONGOLIA
Later under Russian influence

Harbin

SINKIANG
Some British but later Russian
influence predominant

Peking

Dairen
Port Arthur

C H I N A

Lianchow   *Yellow R*

Grand Canal

TIBET
Some British influence

Nanking

Shanghai
Ningpo

Lhasa

Yangtse R

Wenchow
Foochow

Amoy
Formosa (Jap)

Shanghai Treaty ports

Canton   Swatow
Luchow   Hongkong (Br)
West R   Macao (Port)

French influence
British influence
German influence
Russian influence
Japanese influence
++++ Railways

Foreign spheres of influence at the time of the Chinese Revolution

187

3. Battle of the Concessions

The Western powers intervene to prevent Japan acquiring the Liaotung peninsula in Manchuria, then claim their own 'spheres of influence' with exclusive economic and political rights. Control of seaports and concessions to build railways are the key prizes.

Port of Kiaochow (Shantung province) leased to Germany, 1897.

Port Arthur and Liaotung Peninsula leased to Russia, 1898.

Port of Weihaiwei in North China, Kowloon on Chinese mainland opposite Hongkong, both leased to Britain. China promises not to allow other foreign interests in Yangtze valley, 1898.

Kwangchowwan on South China coast leased to France; China promises not to allow other foreign interests in three southern provinces, 1898.

Fukien province opposite Formosa, railway rights in Fukien and three other provinces conceded to Japan, 1900.

4. Dollar Diplomacy

The foreign powers began to realise the danger to their own interests of an unregulated carve-up of China. The rise of Chinese nationalism also compelled them to work in closer co-operation in imposing their demands on China. In 1900 the United States put forward the 'open-door' policy which sought international agreement that China should be open to all foreign trade without special privileges for particular powers. All the powers except Japan, with its eye on Manchuria, came round to this view, although they held on to the 'concessions' they had already obtained. Slowly and painfully the Chinese nationalists won back some of the rights they had lost through the unequal treaties. By the late 1920s they had regained the power to fix their own tariffs; 'extra-territoriality' was not ended until 1943.

But meanwhile China needed foreign loans to pay for the war indemnities imposed upon her, to finance the foreign-built railways and industries, to subsidise the new armies which soon fell into the hands of warlords. Foreign investment encouraged some economic growth in Shanghai, Manchuria and other accessible areas, but the interior lagged behind, widening the gap between town and country-side. Yuan Shih-kai (Extract 17) was the first of many military leaders to strengthen his political position by taking foreign loans. These loans, negotiated with foreign banking consortiums backed by their own governments, carried high rates of interest and China acquired a crippling burden of debt.

Loans: In 1911 41 per cent of all Chinese railways was foreign-owned; it was estimated that it would take China over forty years to buy them back (see Extract 15).

From 1861 to 1937 foreign loans to China were spent as follows: 44 per cent on military expenditure and paying off indemnities; 31 per cent on railways; 20 per cent on government running costs; only 5 per cent for industrial purposes.

In the 1920s between a fifth and a quarter of China's annual revenue was spent on repaying loans.

Investment: After the First World War more money left China in the shape of interest payments and profits than came in through new investments. Every year between 15 and 25 per cent of the total receipts in China's balance of payments went straight out again (See Extract 20).

5. *From Japanese Aggression to American Influence*

Japanese interests in Manchuria and North China steadily grew after her defeat of Russia in the 1904-5 war, and increased further while the Western powers were involved in the First World War.

1931: On the pretext of a small bomb explosion, Japan occupied Manchuria, setting up a puppet state, Manchukuo, in 1932. The League of Nations failed to agree on how to stop Japanese expansion. Japan's control spread into North China and Inner Mongolia.

1937: On another pretext, the 'Marco Polo Bridge' incident, Japan went to war with China, invading Shanghai and capturing the Chinese capital of Nanking. By the end of 1938 Chiang Kai-shek's Nationalist government had retreated to Chungking in the western province of Szechwan. Only Russia provided prompt economic and military aid.

1941: After Pearl Harbor, America declared war on Japan and tried to build up China as a second front. But the area under Nationalist control was cut off from easy communication with the outside world (the Burma Road was only opened in 1945). The war effort was weakened by corruption and collaboration. Only guerrilla units, especially the Chinese communists, fought effectively.

1945: Japan surrendered, the US helped Chiang to regain the Japanese-held areas in northern China. Then after ineffective mediation between Chiang and the Chinese Communists the US backed the Nationalists in the civil war (1946-9), providing 3000 million dollars of economic and military aid.

Further reading

China's relations with the imperialist powers are the subject of numerous monographs based on much diligent investigation in the diplomatic archives, but only the specialist reader is likely to benefit from, for example, a study of Sino-Russian diplomacy, 1878-81. Foreign relations figure prominently in two very readable general studies of modern China, *The Modern History of China* by Henry McAleavy (London: Weidenfeld and Nicolson, 1967, paper), and *China* by Victor Purcell (London: Ernest Benn, 1962). Of the more detailed histories the best and most recent is Immanuel C.Y. Hsu, *The Rise of Modern China* (Oxford University Press, 1970). Roger Pelissier's *The Awakening of China 1793–1949* (Weidenfeld, 1967) contains a lively selection of extracts from original documents. A Chinese interpretation is provided by Hu Sheng, *Imperialism and Chinese Politics* (Peking: Foreign Languages Press, 1955), the source for Extract 10. For some hard analysis of the economic effects of imperialism, consult Chi-Ming Hou, *Foreign Investment and Economic Development in China, 1840–1937* (Harvard University Press, 1965). Han Suyin's three-volume autobiography, *The Crippled Tree – A Mortal Flower – Birdless Summer* (London: Panther, paper) gives a vivid picture of the social implications of the Western assault on China from the vantage-point of someone who, half-Chinese by birth, had a foot in both cultures.

NATIONALISM

The 'Self-Strengthening Movement', 1860s to 1890s. Some Chinese officials, with little support from the imperial court, sought to 'borrow Western techniques to preserve the Chinese way of life'. New armies are set up and equipped, a few students sent abroad, a navy was planned but the funds were appropriated to rebuild the Summer Palace for the Empress Dowager. Leading reformers included the provincial governors Li Hung-chang, Tso Tsung-tang, Chang Chih-tung.

The Reform Movement, 1895-8. Further efforts were stimulated by the Battle of Concessions and Japan's 1895 defeat of China. The Emperor Kuang Hsu, advised by the progressive scholar Kang Yu-wei, tried to reform the bureaucracy, the examination system and the imperial court. His Hundred Days of Reform in 1898 were thwarted by the Empress Dowager, Tzu Hsi (see Extract 13).

The Nationalist Revolution, 1911-12. Two forces combined to over-throw the Manchu dynasty in 1911. Popular opposition to the foreign concessions and the reactionary policies of the imperial court had grown rapidly in the 1900s. Youth, women, merchants, local scholar-officials, workers in new industries, all became more active. Some political leadership was provided by Sun Yat-sen's *Tung-meng-hui* (forerunner of the Kuomintang), mainly composed of foreign-educated students who inspired a number of small revolts but lacked a mass following in China (Extract 16). The second and stronger force was the army, partly affected by revolutionary propaganda, also with its own grievances against the Manchus. General Yuan Shih-kai engineered his appointment as president of the Republic and the new parliament and Constitution soon became his pawns (Extract 17). Yuan's death in 1916 was followed by ten years of war-lordism. The Peking government passed from the hands of one warlord clique to another.

The Northern Expedition, 1927. In the early 1920s Sun Yat-sen's Kuomintang established itself in southern China, stimulated by the rise of nationalism in the May Fourth Movement (Extract 18). Popular boycotts and strikes against the foreign powers helped it to grow. Its political programme was Sun's Three Principles of the People (*San-min chu-yi*):

   Nationalism (anti-imperialism)

   People's Rights (democracy with referendum)

   People's Livelihood (control of capital and economic development).

Sun was impressed by the Russian Revolution, accepted Soviet advisers who helped train the Nationalist army, formed a 'united front' with the newly formed Chinese Communist Party. In 1925 Sun died and was succeeded by Chiang Kai-shek, a powerful young military leader, a Christian, trained in Moscow, and backed by secret societies. In 1926-7 Chiang marched north and more or less unified the country. While doing so he purged and massacred the Com-munists who had helped to gain peasant and workers' support for the Northern Expedition.

Further reading

Apart from the books on the history of modern China referred to in the last section, Lucien Bianco's *Origins of the Chinese Revolution, 1915-1949* (Oxford University Press, 1972) gives a thoughtful account of the nationalist upsurge. Mary Wright provides a more

positive view of the 1911 Revolution than usual in her long introduction to *China in Revolution: The First Phase 1900-1913* (Yale
University Press, 1968). Li Chien-nung's *The Political History of
China 1840–1928* (Stanford University Press, 1967, paper) goes
deep into the warlord politics of the Republic. Jerome Ch'en's
Yuan Shih-k'ai (Allen & Unwin, 1961, Stanford University Press
(revised), 1972) from which Extract 17 is taken gives a lively account
of China's proto-warlord. But a general introduction to the Nationalist
period still has to be written. The first good biography of Sun Yat-sen
was only written in 1970, by Harold Schiffrin (University of California Press), and there is no biography in print of Chiang Kai-shek.
However, there are some useful essays on Nationalist China in Jack
Gray (editor), *Modern China's Search for a Political Form* (Oxford
University Press, 1969). It is worth hunting for second-hand
copies of books by journalists like Edgar Snow, James Bertram,
Agnes Smedley and Robert Payne who wrote from China in the
1930s and 1940s, recording both the heroism of the anti-Japanese
war and the corruption of the Nationalist government, vivid reporting
which has not been bettered by any scholarly product. An earlier
example, which describes the Northern Expedition and Chiang
Kai-shek's purge of the left, is Harold Isaacs's *The Tragedy of the
Chinese Revolution* (New York: Athenaeum, reissued 1966, paper).

COMMUNISM

The Chinese Communist Party (CCP), founded in July 1921, worked
with the Kuomintang from 1923 till it was expelled from the 'united
front' by Chiang Kai-shek in 1927. Mostly composed of urban
intellectuals, it now painfully learnt the same lesson which the
Kuomintang had already absorbed, that in twentieth-century China
no revolutionary political force could survive without military
resources of its own. This is the basic meaning of Mao Tse-tung's
famous statement that 'political power grows from the barrel of a
gun'. While some CCP leaders, hiding in Shanghai, continued to
squabble over how to interpret Stalin's frequent and confusing
directives from the Comintern in Moscow, Mao Tse-tung, Chu Teh
and others took to the hills to organise the first guerrilla Red Army.

The Kiangsi Soviet, 1930-34. Small communist guerrilla forces joined
together to set up a Soviet Government in parts of Kiangsi province,
surviving four Encirclement Campaigns by the Nationalist army.

Then, heavily blockaded and threatened by the fifth campaign, the CCP broke through its encirclement and started the Long March in October 1934. Factional in-fighting among the CCP leadership in which directives from the Comintern continued to play a divisive part, had weakened the Soviet's resistance in Kiangsi. Mao did not gain real political ascendancy until the Tsunyi Conference, held early during the Long March in January 1935.

The Long March, 1934-6. Of the 100,000 men who left Kiangsi in October 1934 less than 10,000 arrived in the north-west province of Shensi a year later, led by Mao Tse-tung and Chu Teh. Armies from other communist areas straggled in later, after disagreements over strategy and direction. Several hundred thousands of Party members and Red Army soldiers had been killed, left the Party or gone underground. But the Long March preserved a tough nucleus for future communist expansion; it also provided an intensive experience of revolutionary struggle and heroism which still inspires the Chinese people today. Mao's First Front Army covered roughly 6000 miles, marching through nine provinces in a vast semicircle which took them to the edge of Tibet, through the head-waters of the Yangtze, over snow-capped mountains and across marshy grasslands. 'The Red Army fears not the trials of a distant march,' wrote Mao when it ended. 'To them a thousand mountains, ten thousand rivers are nothing.'

The Yenan Period, 1937-45. With its capital in Yenan, a remote mountain valley among the loess hills of northern Shensi, the main communist base extended into neighbouring Ninghsia and Kansu provinces. A dozen other 'border areas' grew up later in north and central China. From a few tens of thousands, the Red Army reached a strength of 900,000 by 1945, with two and a half million peasants serving in local militias. After the Sian Incident in December 1936, when Chiang Kai-shek was kidnapped by a patriotic military commander and forced to resist the Japanese more effectively, negotiations led to a second 'united front' between the Nationalists and Communists. The Communists waged guerrilla war against the Japanese, mobilising the peasants behind enemy lines. Still blockaded by the Nationalists, the Communist bases were forced back on their own resources with no external economic or military aid. They also became 'self-reliant' politically, losing almost all contact with the Soviet Union. In the Rectification Campaign (1941-3) Mao led a drive against dogmatism in politics and art. The philosophy of

Marxism-Leninism should be applied concretely to Chinese conditions; popular participation should be encouraged through practising the 'mass line'. Towards the end of the Yenan period, Mao and his colleagues made contact with American officials sent to Yenan to establish liaison for the anti-Japanese war effort. Mao urged the US to stay neutral between Nationalists and Communists, even offering to visit Washington and talk with President Roosevelt. The offer was rejected; against the advice of many of its observers in China, the US took Chiang's side in the coming civil war.

Civil War, 1946-9. By mid-1946 peace negotiations between Nationalists and Communists had broken down. Refusing to let the CCP join in a coalition government, Chiang Kai-shek believed he could wipe them out in a year. In March 1947 he captured Yenan; Mao took to the mountains to organise resistance. But Chiang's lines of communication from north to south were vulnerable; his armies reluctant to fight and over-extended in the Manchurian cities of the north-east. Over four million Nationalist soldiers were to surrender by the end of civil war. The Red Army (now called the People's Liberation Army – still its official name today) grew from one to four million strong. The Communists still received no Soviet aid, relying on home-made weapons and captured American equipment.

Further reading

First, two classics, one old and one new. Edgar Snow visited the Communist base in North-west China (See Extract 22) in 1936, talked at length with Mao Tse-tung and recorded the story of his life, rode and marched with the Red Army and returned to write *Red Star Over China* (Penguin Books, revised edition, 1972). Another American, William Hinton, lived for the spring and summer of 1948 through the process of land reform (see Extract 24) in a North China village, then fell foul of the anti-communist witch-hunt in America and finally published *Fanshen* nearly twenty years later (Penguin Books, 1972). 'Fanshen' literally means 'to turn the body' or 'to turn over', and Hinton describes in a narrative as vivid as fiction how the landless peasants transformed their lives and their social attitudes through the 'struggle' of land reform. Another epic is Agnes Smedley's biography of the Red Army commander Chu Teh, *The Great Road* (Monthly Review Press, 1972, paper). The same press has republished Jack Belden's vivid account of the Civil War, *China Shakes the World* (1970, paper).

The history of the Chinese Communist Party has been better served than that of the Kuomintang. Most of it inevitably centres around the dominating figure of Mao Tse-tung. Jerome Ch'en's *Mao and the Chinese Revolution* (Oxford University Press, 1965, paper) covers the ground thoroughly and has a good chronology. Stuart Schram, *Mao Tse-tung* (Penguin Books, revised 1969), takes the story up to the Cultural Revolution. His *The Political Thought of Mao Tse-tung* (Penguin Books, 1969) provides a 'reader' of key Mao writings. Han Suyin's recent *The Morning Deluge* (London: Jonathan Cape, 1972) accepts the current Chinese version of their Party history, sees Mao as a flawless hero, but conveys quite successfully the epic quality of the revolution. Dick Wilson's *The Long March 1935* (London: Hamish Hamilton, 1971) blends scholarship with narrative. William Sewell's *I Stayed in China* (London: Allen & Unwin) is a gently perceptive account of the Communist take-over in a small Chinese town. C.P. Fitzgerald's *Communism Takes China* (London: Library of the 20th Century, 1971) is concise and well illustrated. So is Robert North's *Chinese Communism* (London: World University Library, 1966).

CONTEMPORARY CHINA

An entirely new interpretation of their recent political history has been made by the Chinese since the Cultural Revolution. Until 1966 when they talked about 'before' and 'after' they referred to life before and after the Liberation of 1949. Now the words refer to the Cultural Revolution itself. Chinese politics since 1949 are described in terms of a continuous political 'struggle between two lines', between the bureaucratic 'revisionist' approach of former Head of State Liu Shao-chi and the revolutionary 'socialist' approach of Mao Tse-tung, which culminated in the Cultural Revolution. Some aspects of this analysis are hard to sustain. But it does make sense to look at Chinese history since 1949 in terms of periods of greater and lesser enthusiasm for the Maoist brand of socialism:

1949-53: Recovery and Reliance. The main task facing the Chinese communists in 1949 was to restore the economy and social unity of a country which had been at war for the past twelve years. At first most of China was administered by the People's Liberation Army which had driven out Chiang Kai-shek's Nationalists. Political power was handed over without apparent difficulty to a dual system of Party Committees and elected People's Governments. The task of reconstruction was complicated by the Korean War in which China was forced to intervene under the threat of General MacArthur's advancing army. But by 1953 inflation had been checked, communications restored, production back to prewar levels, and three million soldiers demobilised. However, the Korean War made China more dependent upon the Soviet Union for aid. The Chinese economy, with thousands of Soviet experts giving advice, was rebuilt with Soviet plant and techniques. The First Five Year Plan, begun in 1953, attached top priority to the development of heavy industry. There was only one political upset – the disgrace and suicide in 1953 of Kao Kang, Communist Party secretary of Manchuria, later accused of secret dealings with the Russians. Inevitably during these first years the mood became less revolutionary, more stolidly socialist in the Soviet style.

1954-7: Consolidation and Re-thinking. In 1954 the first National People's Congress was held and the national Constitution was adopted. The PLA became a conscript army with ranks, medals and sliding pay scale. 'Regularisation' was the slogan; this was the height of the 'Learn from the Soviet Union' campaign. Communist China sometimes seemed to be more 'Communist' – on the lines of the People's Democracies of Eastern Europe – than 'Chinese'. In 1956 the Eighth Party Congress was held, the first since 1945. In the new Party documents Mao Tse-tung's name was hardly mentioned. But there was already some criticism of the Party for being too 'bureaucratic'; of the PLA for being too 'professional'. Mao seemed to come in from the sidelines, once in 1955 when he speeded up collectivisation in the countryside, and again with the Hundred Flowers Campaign of spring 1957 when he encouraged Chinese intellectuals (against the advice of Party leaders) to speak out. There were already hints of a split between the revolutionary and the bureaucratic lines.

1958-65: Great Leap and Setbacks. The goals of the Great Leap Forward, 1958-9, launched by Mao – to steam ahead in agriculture and industry while transforming Chinese society – proved too ambitious. It was followed by three 'lean years' of economic hardship. In September 1959 the Minister of Defence, Peng Teh-huai, was sacked for criticising the Great Leap (see Extract 29) and replaced by Lin Piao. But other leaders still wanted to slow down the pace of revolutionary change. The People's Communes survived but the collective spirit was reduced. In 1962 Mao returned to the offensive with the call: 'Never Forget Class Struggle'. In town and country the Socialist Education Movement was launched to 'clean up' corruption, mismanagement and signs of 'capitalist' behaviour (such as spending more time on privately owned plots than on the collective land). This Movement too got bogged down in the Party's bureaucratic machine, or so Mao Tse-tung believed. In 1963-5 the economy picked up, but everywhere Mao saw signs of the revolution becoming as routine as it had in the Soviet Union.

1966-72: Cultural Revolution and After. The Cultural Revolution operated on two levels; the political struggle in the leadership against Liu Shao-chi and other 'capitalist-roaders', and the mass struggle further down against 'bourgeois' styles of work and behaviour. The two levels sometimes overlapped and came into conflict. Thus the Red Guards started by criticising their own teachers and educational system (Extract 30) but were soon encouraged by Mao to attack the 'power-holders' high up in the Party apparatus. Later on, when the Maoist leadership wanted to end the 'struggle' and start rebuilding the Party, many Red Guards – now described as 'ultra-Left' – tried to carry on (Extract 32). Most recent visitors to China agree that the Cultural Revolution has created a new spirit of self-confidence among ordinary people in China who now feel less overawed of Party authority, more ready to speak up for themselves. But it has had a less happy effect on the leadership where factions have emerged, plots and counter-plots have been discovered. The story of the 'Great Proletarian Cultural Revolution' is far too intricate to relate in detail, but here are the main political forces and individuals on the stage.

Red Guards – mostly secondary-school and college students, began activities in mid-1966. Millions flocked to Peking to see Chairman Mao, encouraged by the Maoist leaders to attack provincial Party and government leaders back in the provinces and set up popular revolutionary committees. But in 1967-8 Red Guards formed rival factions, some with branches all over the country, stole weapons from the PLA, began fighting by force. Finally quelled in late summer 1968, ten million or more were sent to work in the countryside.

Liu Shao-chi – Liu and his wife, Wang Kuang-mei, were the chief individual targets of the Red Guards. Officially described as a traitor who wanted to restore capitalism. In the past more concerned than Mao to stress Party discipline and institutions, wrote *On the Party* and *How to be a Good Communist*. Fate unknown, possibly under house arrest. Other disgraced leaders included Mayor of Peking Peng Chen, Party Secretary-General Teng Hsiao-ping, Minister of Culture Lu Ting-yi, Army Chief of Staff Lo Jui-ching.

People's Liberation Army (PLA) – Since 1959 under Minister of Defence Lin Piao intensively schooled in Mao Tse-tung's Thoughts. *Little Red Book* was first published for the PLA. In 1967 when Party officials intensified opposition against the Cultural Revolution, and Red Guards started fighting, the PLA intervened to keep the peace, but its hands were tied by orders not to use force. July 1967, the Wuhan Incident, when military units in central China tried to kidnap Chou En-lai, but PLA units generally loyal to Mao. PLA officers dominated new 'Revolutionary Committees' set up at all levels, also new 'Party Committees' re-formed after 1968. September

1971, disgrace and probable death of Lin Piao was followed by less emphasis on the PLA's political role.

Lin Piao – proclaimed as Mao's 'chosen comrade-in-arms' and successor during the Cultural Revolution, delivered key political report to the Ninth Party Congress, April 1969. A distinguished military leader from the Long March onwards, commanded the PLA's Manchurian campaign during the 1946-9 civil war. Said to have died in an air crash in Outer Mongolia while fleeing China, September 1971, after a plot against Mao's life. The real story still obscure, perhaps connected with a dispute over economic and defence policies and involving Lin's objection to Mr Nixon's visit to China. Lin is now described as a 'political swindler' who praised Mao to the skies in order to bolster his own authority. Ch'en Po-ta, once Mao's secretary and a leading theoretical writer, also disappeared in 1971 after being condemned as an ultra-leftist.

Chou En-lai – China's Premier, worked hard during the Cultural Revolution to mend fences between rival political factions and prevent Red Guard violence. A tireless worker who receives guests in the early hours of the morning. Sometimes called 'pragmatic' by Western writers, but no evidence that he does not share Mao's socialist vision. However, he has always concentrated on administration and diplomacy and perhaps is more aware of practical limitations. Now very active in China's new diplomacy.

Chiang Ching – Mao's wife, a prominent patron of the Red Guards, sometimes appeared to encourage them to greater defiance. A former film actress, she led the reform of Peking opera, adapting its style to new revolutionary plots. Appears less frequently since 1969, as do other 'leftist' leaders of the Cultural Revolution.

Further reading
The Cultural Revolution with its colourful Red Guard literature, its polemics and clash of ideas, has brought the study of Chinese politics out of the China-Watching doldrums. But the new insight which we now have into leadership and policy differences since 1949 makes most previous studies, none of them very inspiring anyhow, even more lifeless. The general reader is well served by Edgar Snow's 1960 follow-up to his *Red Star* classic, *The Other Side of the River* (Penguin Books, 1970, under the title *Red China Today*), plus the post-1949 section of Stuart Schram's *Mao Tse-tung*. K.S. Karol's *China: The Other Communism* (London: Heinemann, 1967)

based on personal visits supplements Snow for the 1960s. Franz Schurmann's *Ideology and Organization in Communist China* (University of California, revised, 1966, paper) brims with unresolved but interesting questions on how the system works. On the Cultural Revolution ignore all the 'quickies' called 'I Fled from the Red Guards' and suchlike. William Hinton in *Hundred Day War* (Monthly Review, 1972) tells a gripping story of Red Guard factionalism which led to armed fights in Peking's Tsinghua University. Gordon Bennett and Ronald Montaperto, *Red Guard* (New York: Doubleday, 1971) sympathetically interpret the story of just one Red Guard from Canton. Neale Hunter's *Shanghai Journal* (New York: Praeger, 1969) goes deep into one of the most turbulent areas of the Cultural Revolution. Mao Tse-tung's unpublished speeches which surfaced in the Red Guard press have been translated by Jerome Ch'en, *Mao Papers* (Oxford University Press, 1970). (Mao's pre-1949 *Selected Works* are published in four volumes by the Peking Foreign Languages Press. There are some officially published post-1949 speeches and articles by him in various pamphlets and in *Selected Readings from the Works of Mao Tse-tung*).

FOREIGN POLICY

Towards the Soviet Union: February 1950, Sino-Soviet Alliance gave the new People's Republic of China much-needed aid, political and military support against threat of hostile United States. In spite of past lukewarm Soviet attitude towards Chinese revolution, Mao accepted Stalin's leadership of 'socialist bloc'. After the Korean War, China less dependant on the Soviet Union, started to develop more independent foreign policy, Khrushchev regarded by Mao as a weak leader. Russians refused to give nuclear aid to China in late 1950s, only gave half-hearted support in the Offshore Islands and Sino-Indian border crises (1958/9). Also serious ideological disagreements developed; Moscow critical of China's Great Leap Forward, Peking thought Khrushchev soft on US imperialism and uninterested in national liberation movements. Khrushchev withdrew all Soviet aid in 1960, incidents on Sino-Soviet border began in 1962. Soviet signing of the Test-ban Treaty (which denied China the right to make her own nuclear deterrent) led to open split and violent polemics. Mao Tse-tung largely responsible for conduct of policy towards Soviet Union, perhaps tougher than some of his colleagues. China now regards the Soviet Union as a 'super-power', both struggling and collaborating with the United States to dominate the world, actually 'more dangerous' than the US because still deceptively claims to be a socialist state. The Chinese view no doubt influenced by the major border clashes and Soviet threats of war in 1969, followed by fruitless negotiations and massive Soviet military reinforcements.

Towards the United States: Until recently China's attitude was often described as 'intransigent', but the real picture obscured by cold-war writing and anti-China prejudice. In 1949 Peking made overtures for diplomatic recognition to Washington; rejected by the Truman administration which was determined to 'contain' China and thwart revolution elsewhere (the US had already decided to support French colonialism in Indochina to prevent the 'spread of communism'). US and Chinese intervention in the Korean War led to strong US support for Chiang Kai-shek on Formosa. In 1954 after the Korean and Vietnam Wars were settled, China took the initiative in proposing talks with the US, reluctantly accepted by John Foster Dulles, but the Americans refused to discuss relations between the two countries seriously. During the 1960s China felt increasingly threatened by American expansion in South-east Asia and isolated by lack of Soviet support. Frequent US spy-flights, and US-backed commando raids from Taiwan. In the United Nations the US continued to mobilise its bloc vote to keep China from occupying her seat. Finally in 1971 the US accepted the basis on which China had always been willing to negotiate – (1) the Five Principles of Peaceful Co-existence, and (2) military withdrawal from Taiwan, leaving the Chinese Nationalists to settle their differences with the Chinese government in Peking as an internal affair, not a matter for international intervention. In November 1971 China was voted back to the United Nations; Mr Nixon visited Peking in February 1972. As China sees it, US imperialism is more of a 'paper tiger' than ever before; forced to recognise realities by its setbacks in Indochina and by domestic popular pressure.

Towards the Third World: China identifies itself with the ex-colonial developing countries of the Third World all of which it sees as equally threatened by the two 'super-powers'. Does China export revolution? The short answer to this often-asked question is 'no'. China has given some weapons and aid to revolutionary movements elsewhere, but its main export has always been propaganda and the works of Chairman Mao, and the Chinese frequently emphasise that revolutionaries must rely mainly 'on their own resources'. Chinese military aid abroad has been minimal compared with that of the USA, USSR, France or Britain. Yet China is faced with a real problem or 'contradiction'. Should Peking support the *governments* of Third-World countries because they, like China, are opposed to the super-powers? Or should it instead support revolutionary *movements* in these countries (even if only with propaganda), which are struggling against reactionary policies at home? Chinese policies have generally chosen the first alternative. The national revolution, it is argued, must come before the social revolution (just as it did in China). Chinese relations with the Third World were boosted at the Bandung Conference of Asian and African countries in April 1955, expanding rapidly in Africa and the Middle East. Since the Cultural Revolution Chinese diplomatic relations have become much more extensive, including for the first time several countries in Latin America. The whole of the Third World is described by Peking as an 'intermediate zone' of anti-imperialist struggle which separates the super-powers from China.

Towards the West: In the 1950s roughly seventy per cent of China's foreign trade was conducted with the Soviet Union and Eastern Europe, less than thirty per cent with the West (excluding the US which embargoed all trade with China). Today the proportions are reversed. Chinese relations with Western Europe and Canada have improved steadily since the early 1960s; these countries, although capitalist, are seen by Peking as forming a 'second intermediate zone' which in some degree stands up against the super-powers. China approves of the European Economic Community for this reason. Japan, although an Asian power, belongs to the same 'intermediate' category of capitalist countries and is China's biggest trading partner. Peking is concerned at Japan's growing economic and military power, but in 1972, as US–China relations improved, was able to persuade Tokyo to open diplomatic relations.

Further reading

Since Mr Nixon visited China in 1972, the American press has decided that the Chinese are human after all. But read Felix Greene's *A Curtain of Ignorance* (Jonathan Cape, 1965) for a chilling reminder of the years when China was widely portrayed as a nation of starving slaves under the heel of Soviet domination. Three examples of Peking's 'aggression' were usually cited in anti-Chinese propaganda – the occupation of Tibet, the intervention in Korea, and the border war with India in 1962. Gregory Clark, *In Fear of China* (London: Barrie and Rockcliffe, 1968) argues against these and other exaggerated interpretations of Chinese policy. The Korean war is poorly served by scholarship. David Rees, *Korea: the Limited War* (Penguin, 1970) has most of the facts but is wholly uncritical of the Western version in which the communists are assumed to be treacherous throughout and bent on 'world domination'. For a challenging counter-view of Korea and the other major cold-war events see David Horowitz, *From Yalta to Vietnam* (Penguin, 1967). Neville Maxwell's widely praised *India's China War* (Pelican, revised edition, 1972) demolishes the myth that India in 1962 was the victim of unprovoked Chinese aggression. There are good general surveys of Peking's foreign policy in Edgar Snow's *Red China Today* and K.S. Karol's *China: The Other Communism*. Snow played a part in the diplomatic moves leading up to Nixon's Peking visit. Read his last interviews with Mao and Chou En-lai in *The Long Revolution* (London: Hutchinson, 1972).

EDUCATION

The Cultural Revolution has brought about some important changes in China's educational system. The overall length of schooling has been shortened; more time is spent on practical work; more children of workers and peasants are being admitted to higher education. Much of the impetus for reforming education has been provided by Mao Tse-tung. Before the Cultural Revolution he described the system then operating as one which 'strangles talents, destroys young people'. He advocated open-book exams and even suggested that

Students should be permitted to doze off when a lecturer is teaching, Instead of listening to nonsense, they do much better taking a nap to freshen themselves up. Why listen to gibberish anyway? (Speech of 13 February 1964.)

It is doubtful whether education before the Cultural Revolution was as 'élitist' as it is now claimed, but there were more emphasis on purely academic achievement, with streaming and specialisation. Today various regions and schools are trying different experiments to produce a more egalitarian system which will also provide a satisfactory education. The whole system is now (1972) described as 'experimental'.

Primary-school education begins at the age of seven. Formerly six years, its length has generally been reduced to five. Tuition and textbook costs are very low – perhaps ten *yuan* a year. It is not yet universal in all rural areas but its coverage is usually reported to be 80-90 per cent. Some children in remote districts are served by mobile and correspondence classes. There are two terms with a summer holiday of about forty days, a winter holiday of about twenty (usually coinciding with busy farming seasons). Children are likely to spend between three and six weeks in school workshops or local factories and in the countryside. In one Nanking school the curriculum for the fifth grade (11-year-olds) was as follows in 1971:

Chinese language	:	ten periods weekly
Politics	:	four periods
Exercise	:	20 minutes a day
Revolutionary Art	:	two periods
Maths	:	six periods
English	:	two periods
General Knowledge	:	one period

Secondary ('Middle') school education was previously composed of three years in junior-middle and three years in senior-middle, now reduced experimentally to four or five. Generally available in urban areas, less so in the countryside where typical statistics show that some 50 to 60 per cent of primary graduates attend secondary school – mostly only to the end of 'junior-middle'. Subjects include: political studies, history, Chinese, a foreign language (usually English), biology and health (including sex) education, geography, maths, physics and chemistry. Up to two months may be spent doing factory or commune work. Fees are slightly more than at primary school, but there are subsidies. The school day is generally from 8 am to 6.30 pm with an hour's homework.

Primary and secondary schools may be run and financed by city districts, housing estates, factories, rural communes or brigades, or directly by the municipal or county authorities. Textbooks are approved and published by the city or provincial education department. Classes are usually large – forty to fifty – and discipline is strict, though enforced by moral and political persuasion, not by corporal punishment.

Higher education. In universities the courses have generally been shortened from four to three years. Entirely new entrance requirements have been established since the Cultural Revolution. Applicants must:

(a) have two to three years of practical experience working in factories, countryside or armed forces

(b) be recommended by the 'masses' (their fellow-workers)
(c) have graduated from junior-middle school, and satisfy the appropriate educational and political requirements.

Practical work is stressed. Trainee engineers make machine tools,
parts for trucks. Architecture students spend time as construction
workers. Students of hydraulics go to build dams. Some provincial
universities have established 'branch campuses' in the countryside.
Fees and living expenses are paid for by the state. After completing
their course, college graduates will express a preference for their
future employment and this is taken into account when jobs are
assigned. Many institutions are experimenting with open-book
and collective (i.e. including the teacher and the entire class) exams.
Regular group assessments (again including the teacher) are often
made.

Further reading
Many books by recent visitors to China include chapters on edu-
cation and other aspects of Chinese society. Colin Mackerras and
Neale Hunter, two foreign teachers in China just before the Cultural
Revolution, give a first-hand view in *China Observed* (London:
Sphere Books, 1967). R.F. Price, another teacher, has published
Education in Communist China (London: Routledge and Kegan Paul,
1970).

   Contemporary Chinese literature has been well served in the past
by the translations of the Peking Foreign Languages Press, several of
which are used in this volume, but they are hard to get hold of except
through libraries. However, after a dearth during the Cultural
Revolution, it seems likely that titles will start to re-appear – some of
Lu Hsun's stories (see Extract 19) are already available. Collet's
Chinese Gallery (40 Great Russell Street, London WC1) will provide
booklists, or write direct to Guozi Shudian, P.O. Box 399, Peking,
People's Republic of China. The monthly magazine *Chinese Literature*
from Peking has translations of the latest revolutionary writing.
Two other monthlies, *China Pictorial* (mainly illustrated) and *China
Reconstructs* (more text) carry features on modern art and archaeology
as well as on the political and economic side of life in China today.
Some magnificent volumes of art reproductions have been produced
in Peking, illustrating recent discoveries such as those described
in Extract 4. There has been a depressing lack of interest among
Western scholars in post-1949 literature and art, and most work on
the subject is more concerned with the politics than the contents of

contemporary writing. But W.J.F. Jenner's *Modern Chinese Stories* (Oxford Paperbacks, 1970) provides an excellent selection which helps us to see modern China in human terms. The *Poems of Mao Tse-tung* have been published in two volumes by Eastern Horizon Press, Hongkong (1966, and 'Ten More Poems . . .' in 1967).

HEALTH

It has been estimated that before 1949 four million Chinese died each year from infectious and parasitic diseases, sixty million required (but usually did not get) facilities for daily treatment; there were only 12,000 doctors in the country. Since then Chinese medical services have been transformed. In the countryside mass campaigns have greatly reduced the incidence of malaria, schistosomiasis (see Extract 25) and hookworm. Village and street Health Committees have helped to improve sanitation thus checking the spread of infectious and gastro-intestinal diseases. Venereal diseases have been almost eliminated – the 'preventive' measure in this case was mainly the ending of prostitution.

Many communes have their own hospitals with fixed or mobile clinics at the brigade level. The best facilities are still in the cities but since 1965 there has been a campaign to persuade medical workers to move to the countryside. 'The focus of medical and public health work,' said Mao Tse-tung, 'should be transferred to the villagers'. Large numbers of 'barefoot doctors' – paramedical workers able to make simple diagnoses, deliver babies, teach contraception etc – have been trained from the rural areas.

Health is not free although most costs are borne by the state or local authorities. Peasants usually belong to a commune insurance scheme paying about one *yuan* (20p) a month. Workers usually have free coverage; their families receive a 50 per cent subsidy. Drugs and medicines are cheap, and a visit to the doctor may only cost one-tenth of a *yuan*.

Birth-control methods include the pill, the coil, the sheath and (infrequently) vasectomy and abortion. These are supplied free of charge. Women are encouraged not to marry before 25; men not before 28. Social pressures are more effective in enforcing this policy of 'late marriage' in the towns than in the countryside. Women workers are entitled to fifty-six days of maternity leave on full pay. Most offices, big shops etc. have a crèche where babies can be minded and fed during working hours. In the countryside women may resume light work after thirty days; rural communities also run their own crèches. Children receive free immunisation for TB, smallpox, whooping cough, polio, measles, encephalitis and meningitis. Most visitors to China today, especially those with experience of other Third World countries, are struck by the absence of visible child ailments.

Doctors of traditional and Western-style medicine practise together in Chinese hospitals. The traditional doctors, who outnumber the others by six to one, employ herbal medicines and acupuncture. In acupuncture, needles are used to puncture and stimulate points at various positions and depths on the body which in turn affect other tissues and organs, the relationship between points and organs having been established by long experience. It produces particularly good results for illnessses of the nervous system, but it is also now used to anaesthetise patients undergoing some form of surgery.

Further reading
Joshua Horn, *Away with all Pests* (Monthly Review, 1969, paper), an English surgeon with long experience in China, gives a fascinating account from the inside. Entirely new ground is broken by Ruth Sidel, *Women and Child Care in China* (New York: Hill and Wang, 1972), based on recent on-the-spot investigations. The Peking Foreign Language Press has published (1971) a small pamphlet on *Acupuncture Anaesthesia*. Health and education before the Cultural Revolution are both dealt with in Felix Greene's *The Wall Has Two Sides* (London: Jonathan Cape, 1962, paper).

AGRICULTURE

Eighty per cent of the Chinese population lives on the land. The vast majority except for those in some 'national minority' areas (see Extract 26) live in People's Communes which were set up during the Great Leap Forward in 1958-9. Before then the rural areas went through the following stages:

1949-52 Land reform: Land was taken from the landlords and rich peasants, leaving them with small holdings, and redistributed. In areas already under control of the communists this had begun during the civil war (1946-9, see Extract 24).

1952-3 Mutual-aid teams: Ten or so peasant households joined together to share manpower, farm tools etc. in busy seasons and later all the year round.

1953-5 Semi-socialist Agricultural Producers' Co-operatives (APCs):
Several times larger than the mutual-aid teams. Part of the produce
was shared according to the size of each family's holding, part
according to the amount of work performed, but titles were retained
and tax was paid individually.

1955-7 Fully-socialist APCs: Directly encouraged by Mao Tse-tung,
land became collective property, animals and tools purchased from
their owners by the co-operative, income distributed according to the
number of workdays put in by members.

1958-on People's Communes: Larger than the co-operatives, able to
develop 'diversified economies' (setting up small industries, fishing,
forestry etc.), the lowest unit of government. After some over-
ambitious experiments during the Great Leap which included
communal eating and abolition of 'private plots' (see below), settled
down to the following form essentially unchanged since then.

There are about 74,000 people's communes in China. They are
divided into three 'levels of organisation', the commune, the brigade
and the team. The commune is responsible for big projects like tractor
stations, irrigation works, farm machinery repair shops, secondary
schools. A typical commune might have a population of 20,000 to
50,000 people, some as little as 10,000. The brigade is responsible
for smaller projects including small reservoirs, primary schools and
health clinics. There may be twenty or so brigades in an average-
size commune, or as few as ten. The team is about the size of a small
village with one or two hundred inhabitants. This is the main level
of organisation. The team keeps its own accounts and registers the
'work-points' earned by each household. At the year's end it has a
'share-out' of its income. It must sell a fixed quota of its produce to
the state and pay agricultural tax (less than seven per cent), and
usually makes a contribution to brigade funds. The remainder is
divided between investment for new equipment, collective savings,
and income for members. Households usually have small 'private
plots' where they can raise poultry or grow vegetables. In some
communes where the teams are very small, or where the principal
crop is a cash one (e.g. tea), the brigade and not the team is the basic
financial unit where these decisions are taken. Here is a typical
'share-out' of a tea-producing brigade near Hangchow:
Household distribution – 60 per cent
Agricultural tax – 8 per cent (slightly higher for commercial crop)
Reserve fund – 13 per cent   Equipment, etc. – 19 per cent

Further reading

Jan Myrdal spent a month in a relatively poor Chinese village near Yenan, conducted fifty interviews with local leaders and ordinary peasants. His first book, *Report from a Chinese Village* (Penguin Books, 1967) joins the select group of 'classics' with Snow's *Red Star* and Hinton's *Fanshen* (see under Communism). Two Australians, E.L. Wheelwright and Bruce McFarlane, have frequently visited China. Their *The Chinese Road to Socialism* (New York: Monthly Review Press, 1970) covering industrial and agricultural policy is one of the few books by professional economists to give due credit to Chinese achievements. Keith Buchanan's *The Chinese People and the Chinese Earth* is a very readable and sympathetic introduction to China's geographical economy. For a useful reference book, consult T.R. Tregear's *A Geography of China* (University of London Press, 1965). There are a number of recent pamphlets on China's geography and economic 'models' like Tachai (Shansi province) from the Peking Foreign Languages Press.

STATISTICS

Production: China has issued very few statistics since the Great Leap Forward when some highly exaggerated estimates were published which then had to be scaled down. But some figures have been provided for 1970-71. The following table shows the figures for 1970, with real or percentage increases for 1971 in brackets:

Value of industrial output: US $90,000 million (10%)

Value of agricultural output: US $30,000 million

Crude oil production: over 20 million tons (27.2%)

Steel production: about 18 million tons (21m. tons)

Chemical fertilisers: about 14 million tons (20.2%)

Cotton production: 8500 million linear metres

Grain production: over 240 million tons (246m. tons) (about the same in 1972).

The growth of rural-based local industry is strongly encouraged, and in 1971 the output of small chemical fertiliser plants and cement works accounted for 60 and 40 per cent respectively of the national total.

It appears that since 1957 China has had an annual growth rate of about four to five per cent for industrial production and three per cent for agriculture. The increase in grain production has just kept pace with the increase in population but there is a greater variety of other foods. A few million tons are imported each year although some rice is also exported. However these estimates of economic growth do not take into account China's very substantial investment in health, education, leisure amenities and other 'human resources' which do much to raise the standard of living and also provide an essential basis for future economic growth.

Finance and Wages

Over eighty per cent of China's national revenue comes from profits and taxes of state-owned industrial and commercial enterprises, about seven per cent from the agricultural tax paid by rural people's communes. Some urban land and houses may still be owned privately and taxed. The remaining income comes from taxes on co-operative enterprises, licence fees (e.g. for bicycles), etc. There is no personal income tax.

The exchange is over five *yuan* to the pound sterling, but differences in the cost of living make straight comparisons of prices difficult. A family with two children in an urban area can manage adequately with an income of 100 *yuan* a month, which usually means that both husband and wife work. Housing (probably a two-room flat with shared kitchen and lavatory) will not cost more than four or five *yuan*. Basic foods, cereals and vegetables, are cheap, meat and fish more expensive. Total monthly food costs may be fifteen to eighteen *yuan* per adult. There is rationing for rice or other grains, cotton and sometimes fuel. In the countryside a similar family may only earn 300 *yuan* a year in cash, but it will receive its regular share of grain and other produce from the commune. Here are three typical examples of monthly wages:

(a) Nanking Fertiliser Plant:

Highest — 107 *yuan* (120 for technicians)
Average — 55 *yuan*
Unskilled — 34 *yuan*

(b) A Peking Middle School:

Highest — 150 *yuan* (for experienced teachers)
Average — 70 *yuan*
Lowest — 46 *yuan* (for new teachers)

(c) Shanghai Docks:

Highest — 96 *yuan* (worker or management)
Average — 72 *yuan*
Lowest — 44 *yuan*

Defence

The Chinese armed forces are roughly three million strong. Most able-bodied men and women belong to the local militia, but not more than thirty million of these throughout the nation actually have weapons. Conscription is selective – there are more eligible recruits each year than the People's Liberation Army actually needs, so it can take its pick. Conscripts spend three years in the army, or four in the air force, or five in the navy. Officers and NCOs are 'regulars', but they live almost as simply as the recruits. Pay is low by civilian standards: an officer with six years' service may only get twenty *yuan* a month. Since 1965 when formal ranks and other distinctions were abolished, officers' uniforms have been almost the same as those of the men (but two more pockets, and slightly better material). Officers are now known by their function ('Commander of X unit', or 'Chief of Staff of Y Region') not as previously by a fixed rank ('Colonel' or 'Captain', etc.).

Not many divisions of the Chinese army are mechanised; armoured divisions are also few. A great deal of emphasis is still placed on moving fast, on one's own feet. In training soldiers as much importance is attached to political motivation as to technical expertise. 'Serving the people' by doing non-military work (soldiers keep pigs and grow their own vegetables) is also stressed, but less so now than in the revolution. The army is basically well equipped, especially with Chinese-made light weapons, and Western experts have a healthy respect for it.

The navy is small and mostly concerned with coastal defence. It has far fewer modern ships than, for example, the Japanese navy, and it could not transport large numbers of troops overseas. But it has a growing submarine fleet constructed in Chinese shipyards. The air force has also been concerned much more with defence than offence, with up-to-date Soviet-style MIG-fighters (now built in China) but obsolete sub-sonic bombers. China's nuclear programme got under way in 1958 when it was decided that the Soviet 'nuclear umbrella' could no longer be relied on. By the end of 1972 there had been fifteen tests of atomic and thermonuclear bombs, and China is likely to have inter-continental missiles within a few years. The Chinese regard nuclear weapons as a necessary means of defence against the two great nuclear powers, the US and the Soviet Union. But they still believe that nuclear weapons are 'paper tigers' (see Extract 23) in the sense that such weapons cannot be used to prevent social progress and revolution from continuing to develop.

211

Population

Estimated growth:

1350	—	60 million	1950	—	550 million
1750	—	180 million	1965	—	730 million
1850	—	430 million	1972	—	800 million

Population continues to grow by roughly two per cent annually, although the Chinese themselves admit that their figures are far from precise. A recent study is Leo Orleans, *Every Fifth Child: The Population of China* (London: Eyre Methuen, 1972).

LANGUAGE

The Chinese written language has developed from the earliest pictographs some 3500 years ago to the more stylised and complicated characters (one 'character' or symbol equals one single-syllabled word) in use today. Many characters are combinations of older and simpler ones, containing elements which indicate the meaning, or the sound, or both. To read a Chinese newspaper one needs to know three to four thousand characters; a scholar of classical literature may need to recognise at least ten thousand.

Chinese characters have the advantage that (although they contain some phonetic elements) they basically identify the *meaning*, not the *sound*, of each word. So however differently a word is pronounced it is written exactly the same way. A Cantonese and a northerner, for example, will find it easier to communicate in writing than in speech. But learning characters is a slow process and it has obvious disadvantages for printing, telegrams and other forms of communication. Since 1949 the Chinese have produced lists of officially approved 'simplified characters' – reducing the number of individual strokes needed to write many of the more complicated characters. However the ultimate aim is to replace the characters (except for purposes of scholarly work) by a phonetic script. The system of *Hanyu Pinyin* ('Chinese Phonetics') has been taught in some Chinese schools experimentally and it is used in textbooks for foreign students of Chinese. But a phonetic script will only be generally comprehensible if differences in the spoken language are not too great. All children are now taught at school to speak the 'national language' (or Mandarin) but it will be many decades before major dialect differences are overcome. Richard Newnham's *About Chinese* (Penguin, 1971) gives a clear picture of this, for most Westerners, very muddling subject.

ACKNOWLEDGEMENTS AND SOURCES

I wish to thank the following for permission to reprint: Penguin Books Ltd for Extract 2 from Professor D. C. Lau's *Mencius*; George Allen & Unwin Ltd for Extract 9 from Arthur Waley's *The Opium War Through Chinese Eyes*; Hutchinson & Co. for Extract 16 from Sun Yat-sen's *Memoirs of a Chinese Revolutionary*; Dr Jerome Ch'en for Extract 17 from his *Yuan Shih-k'ai*; *The China Quarterly* for Extract 18 from Mao's 'Great Union of the Popular Masses'; the University of British Columbia (Pacific Affairs) for Extract 20 from *Agrarian China*; Mr Frank Coe, executor for Anna Louise Strong's estate, Extract 23; the *Far Eastern Economic Review* (Hongkong), for Extracts 32 and 33; and Mr A. Z. Obaidullah Khan for Extract 34. I have provided full bibliographical details for the above extracts in the complete list below of sources to all the translations used in this volume. No question of copyright arises in the case of translations published in China, but the reader will see that I have made extensive use of these. I owe a great debt of gratitude to both the unnamed and the named translators (among the latter particularly to Yang Hsien-yi and Gladys Yang) who have done so much to introduce China, its society, culture and literature, to a Western audience in the past two decades.

Extracts:
1. 'The Northern Hills', from *Shih Ching (The Book of Songs)* translated in a selection by Yang Hsien-yi and Gladys Yang, *Chinese Literature* (Peking), March 1962.
2. Chang Chi-hsien, 'Tyrant and Scholars' (from *Lo-yang chin-shen chiu-wen-chi*) in W.W. Yen, *Stories of Old China* (Peking: Foreign Languages Press (FLP), 1958), pp. 60–5.
3. *Mencius*, Book 1, Part A, 7, translated by D.C. Lau (Penguin Classics, 1970), pp. 54–9, copyright © D.C. Lau, 1970.
4. 'Rare Archaeological Find', *China Pictorial* (Peking), October 1972.
5. Wang An-shih, 'Thoughts', translated by Yang Hsien-yi and Gladys Yang, *Chinese Literature*, November 1965.
6. Shih Nai-an, *Heroes of the Marshes*, from chapter 16, translated by Sidney Shapiro, *Chinese Literature*, October 1963, pp. 66–72.
7. Chou Shih-teh, 'Ma Chun – Third Century Mechanical Engineer', *China Reconstructs* (Peking), August 1964.
8. Hsiang Ta, 'A Great Chinese Navigator', *China Reconstructs*, July 1956.
9. Arthur Waley, *The Opium War through Chinese Eyes* (London: Allen & Unwin, 1958), pp. 28–31.
10. Hu Sheng, *Imperialism and Chinese Politics* (Peking: FLP, 1955), pp. 18–23.

11.   Robert Swinhoe, *Narrative of the North China Campaign of 1860* (London: Smith, Elder & Co., 1861), pp. 389–91.

12.   The Cuba Commission, *Report of the Commission Sent by China to Ascertain the Condition of Chinese Coolies in Cuba* (Shanghai: Imperial Maritime Customs Press, 1876), pp. 3–4, 6, 7, 18–19, 86.

13.   *The Emperor Kuang Hsu's Reform Decrees, 1898* (Peking: North-China Herald Office, 1900), pp. 14, 16, 44.

14.   'The Iron Man', from 'Folk Tales of the Boxers Uprising', translated by Gladys Yang, *Chinese Literature*, January 1960, pp. 96–8, 102–5.

15.   Hsu Chi-heng, 'The Man who Built the First Chinese Railway', *China Reconstructs*, July 1955.

16.   Sun Yat-sen, *Memoirs of a Chinese Revolutionary* (London: Hutchinson & Co., 1927), pp. 199, 202–3, 219–24.

17.   Dr Jerome Ch'en, *Yuan Shih-k'ai* (Stanford University Press, 1972, revised with new material), pp. 158, 173–6, copyright © Jerome Ch'en, 1972.

18.   Mao Tse-tung, 'The Great Union of the Popular Masses', translated by Stuart R. Schram, *The China Quarterly* (London: Contemporary China Institute), no. 49, January-March 1972, pp. 80–2, 87.

19.   Lu Hsun, 'An Incident', from *Selected Stories of Lu Hsun*, translated by Yang Hsien-yi and Gladys Yang (Peking: FLP, 1960, reissued 1972), pp. 65–7.

20.   Hsu Yung-sui, 'Tobacco Marketing in Eastern Shantung', *Shun-Pao Weekly Supplement* (Shanghai), II.14, translated in *Agrarian China*, compiled and translated by the Research Staff of the Secretariat, Institute of Pacific Relations (London: Allen & Unwin, 1939), pp. 171–5.

21.   Mao Tse-tung, 'The Foolish Old Man who Removed the Mountains' (11 June 1945), *Selected Works of Mao Tse-tung*, Vol. III (Peking: FLP, 1965), p. 322.

22.   Fan Tse-ai, 'Collecting Medicinal Herbs', *The Long March, Eyewitness Accounts* (Peking: FLP, 1963), pp. 179–83.

23.   Anna Louise Strong, 'A World's Eye View from a Yenan Cave (An Interview with Mao Tse-tung)', *Amerasia* (New York), 19 April 1947, pp. 122–6.

24.   Ting Ling, *The Sun Shines Over the Sangkan River*, translated by Yang Hsien-yi and Gladys Yang, *Chinese Literature*, January 1953, pp. 257–63, (also Peking: FLP, 1954).

25.   Pan Yueh, 'Ending the Scourge of Schistosomiasis', *China Reconstructs*, August 1957.

26.   Fei Hsiao-tung and Lin Yueh-hwa, 'Ways of Life among China's Minorities', *China Reconstructs*, April 1957.

27.   Chou Li-po, *Great Changes in a Mountain Village*, Vol. I, translated by Derek Bryan (Peking: FLP, 1961), pp. 220–4, 226–8.

28.   Mao Tse-tung, 'Reply to Comrade Kuo Mo-jo' (9 January 1963), *Chinese Literature*, May 1966.

29.   Chen Kuang-sheng, 'Why Millions Honour Lei Feng', *China Reconstructs*, June 1963.

30.   Peking No. 1 Girls' Middle School, Letter to Central Committee and Chairman Mao – 'Strongly Urging Abolition of Old College Entrance Examination System', *China Reconstructs*, October 1966.
31.   Wang Kuan-hua, 'Don't Want New Jackets or Leather Shoes', *China Reconstructs*, April 1967.
32.   *Sheng-wu-lien*, 'Whither China' manifesto, extract in *Far Eastern Economic Review* (Hongkong), 3 October 1968, p. 74.
33.   Hsu Shih-yu, speech of 11 June 1968, source as Extract 32.
34.   Hsu Chung-chi, Introduction to Feng Shen Street Committee, in *The Yellow Sand-hills and the Street of the Plentiful*, compiled by K.M. Kaiser, A.Z. Obaidullah Khan, Riaz Mohammed Khan (mimeographed, 1972).

Illustrations:

The battle on the bridge (page 2) and disciples of Confucius (p. 16), from the *Wu-liang-ch'i* stone slabs (*Chin-shih-suo* edition); Two Emperors (pp. 6–7), from the Imperial Palace collection (*Ku-kung Chou-k'an*, 1932); Ma Yuan's Confucius (p. 13), from a recent Chinese print; Acrobats (p. 20), from Liu Chih-yuan's collection of Han tomb tiles (Peking, 1958); Rice-planting (p. 23), and throwing the silk (p. 34), from a Kanghsi edition of the *Geng Chih T'u* (Jung-pao-chai woodblock collection, Peking, 1958); Heroes of the Marshes (p. 29), from Ch'en Ch'i-ming's collection of Ming illustrations (Peking, 1955); dragon's backbone (p. 35) from the 17th-century edition of the *T'ien-kung K'ai-wu* collection; Cheng Ho (p. 40), from a Ming illustration to the novel by Lo Mou-teng (*China Reconstructs*, July 1956); Canton print (p. 46), by H. Melville, 1845 (author's possession); tract (pp. 48–9), from *The Chinese Opium-Smoker* (London, Partridge, n.d.); magistrate's court (p. 52), from A.J. Hardy's *John Chinaman at Home* (London, 1905); allied invasion (p. 58 bottom), from a contemporary Chinese colour print; Taku Fort (p. 58 top), from the source of Extract 11; missionaries (p. 61), from W.E. Geil, *A Yankee on the Yangtze* (London, 1904); Tzu Hsi Dowager (p. 66), from Bland and Backhouse's *China under the Empress Dowager* (London, 1910); Boxers (p. 70), from a contemporary British print (Radio Times Hulton Picture Library); railway scene (pp. 76–7), from the *Tien-shih-chai hua-pao* (Shanghai, 1884); Sun Yat-sen (p. 82) and Yuan Shih-k'ai (p. 87), from Radio Times Hulton Picture Library; May Fourth scenes (p. 91), from Sidney Gamble, *Peking* (London, 1921); Lu Hsun (p. 96), from Camera Press Ltd; 1930s' woodcuts (pp. 102–3), from a selection of Lu Hsun's collection (Peking, 1963); New Year thanks (p. 110) and struggle session (p. 122), from an album of New Year wall-posters (Shanghai, 1950); the assault on feudalism (p. 120) and minority women (p. 132), from *Shih-nian-lai pan-hua hsuan-chi* (Shanghai, 1960); Red Guard cartoons (pp. 154–5), in the author's possession; revolutionary poster (p. 158), from source for Extract 31; back cover from a paper-cut in the author's possession.

The front cover and all photographs of China in the 'Contemporary China' section (pp. 106, 114, 128, 140, 145, 149, 160, 161, 163, 166, 167, 171) were taken by Richard and Sally Greenhill during a visit in April 1971.

The maps on pp. 174 and 187 were drawn by Specialised Drawing Services.